The Best of British
Illustration and Photography

Compiled by The Association of Illustrators
and the Association of Fashion, Advertising
and Editorial Photographers

Edited by Jacqueline Hollister and Alison Theaker
Designed by Adrian Hodgkins

BEST OF BRITISH

Michael Webb

RotoVision

Illustrations compiled by
The Association of Illustrators
1 Colville Place, Off Charlotte Street, London W1P 1HN

Photographs compiled by
The Association of Fashion, Advertising and Editorial Photographers
9–10 Domingo Street, London EC1Y 0TA

Publisher
RotoVision S.A.
10 Rue de l'Arquebuse, 1211 Geneva, Switzerland

Co-ordinator
Marjorie Gordon-Box
2 St. John's Lane, London EC1

Illustrations Photography
Colin Barker
Unit 1A, 6A Pratt Street, London NW1 0AB

Typeset in Great Britain by Joshua Associates Ltd, Oxford
Printed in Japan

First published 1987

ISBN 2-88046-065-4

Jacket picture: Brush and Rainbow Drop by Julian Nieman

CONTENTS

INTRODUCTION

The *Best of British* brings together outstanding work featured in the two prestigious exhibitions organised annually by the Association of Illustrators and the Association of Fashion, Advertising and Editorial Photographers. This unique publishing venture provides the first handy reference guide to the best contemporary British photography and illustration in a single volume. It aims to make the achievements of illustrators and photographers accessible to a new, wider audience. This should help them gain the recognition they deserve outside the narrow confines of the industry in which they work.

The collection contains a bewildering variety of styles, techniques, media and subjects. The pictures shown here have been used in advertising campaigns, on book covers, record sleeves, calendars, packaging, magazine illustrations and in many other ways. But most of them, including some of the pictures in the sections of unpublished, personal work, were created within the discipline of a brief. They were intended to communicate specific messages beyond their creators' private, subjective feelings. They are extrovert images, intended to be seen and readily understood by as many people as possible.

Yet one of the joys of looking through this book is that the pictures are also aesthetically successful. They comment with perception and wit on social conventions, artistic trends and political and moral issues. They entertain and amuse at the same time as they inform and persuade.

Another thread holding these pictures together is that they are fleeting. They are brief, bright flashes in the whirl of change that is the image-making industry. Nothing stands still. A campaign that influences millions one month is forgotten the next.

Yet paradoxically, it will probably be by these images that future ages will remember ours. The pictures contained in this book reflect the flavour of our time. The Best of British forms an enduring cultural record of a brief moment in this process. It allows us to pause and enjoy the artistry and brilliance that go into filling our lives with new images every day.

But it also points forward. The student work included in the book, together with the sections of previously unpublished, experimental work of established artists and photographers, reveal visual trends that will affect the market and the industry in the future.

There are few books to rival the Best of British as a reference guide, talent finder and a source of ideas and inspiration for those involved in communication anywhere in the world.

But all of these uses will probably take second place to the sheer pleasure of turning the pages and admiring the skill, inventiveness, perception and hard work that have gone into making these pictures the visual feast they are.

IMAGES 11 CONTENTS

INTRODUCTION

In 1973 the Association of Illustrators was formed to protect the rights of illustrators and promote contemporary illustration. Membership to the AOI is open to anyone producing or commissioning illustration, art directors, artists' agents, tutors and students and of course professional illustrators. The organisation is constantly expanding its activities, now serving over 1,000 members.

The policies set by the illustrators, clients and agents serving on the AOI committee are implemented by the Association's three full-time administrators. They are always available in the office and on the telephone to give advice to members about contracts, fees, copyright laws and professional ethics . . . and just plain support when it's needed. The AOI will also answer requests for illustrators' addresses and telephone numbers and can assist clients in finding the illustrator they need by directing them to the Annuals and to the AOI slide bank of members' work – Image File.

The Association publishes the lively and topical *Illustrators*, a quarterly magazine sent to members and subscribers. Also free to members is the monthly newsletter with the latest from the industry, listings of exhibitions and lectures and details of special services on offer to them through the AOI.

Situated off Charlotte Street in the heart of London, the AOI Gallery is amidst publishing houses, advertising agencies and design groups, and is easily accessible for agents, clients and the public who come to view the work of the established and newcomers in illustration. Amongst other exhibitions in 1986 the gallery hosted several book launches which proved highly successful for the publishers and illustrators involved. The Association also organises its own exhibitions when members are invited to submit and hopefully sell their work.

Two sponsored competitions are organised by the AOI every year, culminating in major exhibitions in the autumn. The Benson and Hedges Photographers' and Illustrators' Gold Awards give students and professionals the chance to compete for cash prizes and a place in the London exhibition and nationwide tour, by interpreting a one-word theme. The Young Illustrators' competition sponsored by *The Reader's Digest* offers students and those recently out of college the opportunity to produce a set of illustrations for one of three selected books. The resulting exhibition of successful entries has over the years proved instrumental in launching new talent into the industry.

Sponsored Awards

The AOI receives generous sponsorship from five companies who support awards in the Annual Exhibition. Each company selects an artist to receive their award, and a cash prize at the opening of the exhibition. The 1986 sponsored awards are as follows:
The Beresford Sherman Award for the Best Unpublished Work
The Creative Review Award for the Best Use of Humour
The DRG/Royal Sovereign DeVilbiss Award for Excellence in the Use of Airbrush
The Fitch Award for the Most Promising Newcomer
The Rexel Cumberland Award for the Best Coloured Pencil Illustration

Acknowledgements

The AOI wishes to thank the following people who have contributed to *Images 11, The Best of British*, annual and exhibition: the 1986 AOI committee, Mick Bray, chairman, Susan Alcantarilla, John Bendall, Katherine Greenwood, Tessa Land, Mark Urgent, and in particular Steven Wells of the Images sub-committee, for their time and effort; the AOI administration, Anne Bain, Jacqueline Hollister and Vicki Rogers for their unfailing support and hard work; Sarah Culshaw and Tim Woolgar for their advice even beyond the call of duty and all those other AOI supporters who have given generously of their time.

The information in the captions varies according to the length and accuracy of the material supplied by the artist, agent or client. Accordingly, some captions are more detailed than others.

ADVERTISING

Dan Fern

Title
Xerox Collage
Commissioned by
David Dalley
Agency
Young & Rubicam
Client
Rank Xerox

The brief for this illustration was to produce a collage painting using the reduction and enlargement facilities of the Rank Xerox 1025 colour copier and demonstrating its ability to reproduce brightness of colour when copying.

Painting, collage using photocopies. 60 × 90 cms.

Paul Allen

Title
Computers
Commissioned by
Henri Impers
Agency
Publicis Intermarco
Client
Philips Computers

The artist had to show the combination of different component elements making up a whole, which can be adapted or added to, according to needs. The brief required that this be done without including any actual computer hardware.

Computer graphics, airbrush.
42 × 58 cms.

LA CRAIE

James Marsh

Title
Napoleon on Horseback
Commissioned by
Graham Watson
Agency
Bartle Bogle Hegarty
Client
Courvoisier

The artist was asked to produce a
pastiche after David, of
Napoleon on horseback holding
a glass of cognac.

Acrylic on canvas board.
50 × 40 cms.

James Marsh

Title
Napoleon's Nose
Commissioned by
Graham Watson
Agency
Bartle Bogle Hegarty
Client
Courvoisier

The artist was asked to produce a pastiche after David, of Napoleon sniffing a glass of cognac.

Acrylic on canvas board.
50 × 40 cms.

Simon Edwards

Title
A Fine Performance
Commissioned by
Steve Hicks and Glynn Hayes
Agency
Hicks and Hayes
Client
AKAI (U.K.) Ltd

An illustration was required to promote a new range of special effects sound recorders; the machines stack in a modular fashion, one on top of the other.

Photo-collage, watercolour.
42 × 29 cms.

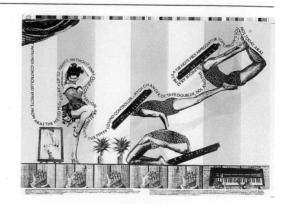

Bill Kennedy

Title
Van Gogh
Commissioned by
Kevin Jones
Agency
Lowe Howard Spink Marschalk
Client
Whitbread & Co PLC

This illustration was a continuation of the 'Heineken refreshes the parts other beers cannot reach' campaign. The artist was asked to use the style of Van Gogh.

Oil. 51 × 75 cms.

Larry Learmonth

Title
Wet Zebra
Commissioned by
Derek Hass
Agency
Lowe Howard Spink Marschalk
Client
Shell Petroleum

The artist was asked to illustrate dramatically the obvious dangers of a wet 'zebra crossing'. The danger subsides when treated with a Shell bi-product.

Oil. 61 × 76 cms.

Allan Manham

Title
Monarch
Commissioned by
Stuart Baker
Agency
Abbot Mead Vickers/SMS Ltd
Client
Glenlivet

The artist was asked to produce a
court portrait of George IV
depicted as a secret drinker.

Oil. 60 × 70 cms.

Peter Till

Title
Wall Street
Commissioned by
Kim Richmond
Agency
Brookes & Vernons (Midlands)
Ltd
Client
Tandem Computers

The artist was asked to illustrate graphically the confusion that would occur in Wall Street if its principal computer systems were removed (i.e. knotted skyscrapers). The illustration was used for advertisements in the national press and for posters.

Pen and ink. 40 × 50 cms.

Peter Till

Title
Tightrope Walker
Commissioned by
Chris Terry
Agency
McCann Erickson Advertising
Ltd
Client
Ashton Tate

The artist was asked to construct an image to accompany the line "Database III strikes the impossible balance", referring to the difficulty in getting the right balance when choosing a computer.

Pen and ink, watercolour.
30 × 30 cms.

Paul Leith

Title
Choose Your Poison
Commissioned by
Guy Moore
Agency
Legas Delaney Partnership
Client
The Point, Milton Keynes

The artist was given an open brief for this illustration of a bar scene which was for one of a series of posters for The Point, Milton Keynes.

Acrylic. 72 × 51 cms.

David Sim

Title
After a Mystery Film
Commissioned by
Guy Moore
Agency
Legas Delaney Partnership
Client
The Point, Milton Keynes

The artist was given an open brief for this illustration which was for one of a series of posters for The Point, Milton Keynes. The illlustration had to be of a restaurant scene and include a steak.

Watercolour, ink. 38 × 25.5 cms.

Chris McEwan

Title
Gardens and Gardeners
Commissioned by
Judith Cole
Client
The British Council

A poster and catalogue cover were required for an exhibition promoting British books on gardens. The exhibition was to tour several countries outside Britain and so the illustration had to reflect one popular type of British garden in a witty and colourful way.

Gouache. 30 × 42 cms.

Alison Wisenfeld

Title
Festival of Paperbacks,
Summer '85
Commissioned by
Richard Boxall for John Midgley
Client
Blackwell Scientific Publications
Ltd

The artist was asked to produce
an illustration for the poster and
catalogue cover used to promote
Blackwell's summer sale of
paperbacks.

Watercolour. 29.5 × 40.5 cms.

Graham Philpot

Title
The 'Winter' One Day Travel
Card.
Commissioned by
Tim Peckett
Agency
Foote Cone & Belding Ltd
Client
London Transport

This is an illustration for one of a
series of posters required for
Underground stations and bus
shelters. The brief was to provide
a border illustration to a poem,
reflecting the 1930's feel but
depicting activities of today in
London, in this instance during
the winter time.

Inks. 37 × 59 cms.

Wilson McLean

Title
Pillar Box
Commissioned by
Michael Bennallack-Hart
Agency
McCann Erickson Advertising
Ltd
Client
The Post Office

The artist was asked for a free interpretation based on the idea of letters flying into a pillar box.

Oil. 60 × 70 cms.

David Hockney

Title
The Castle Race
Commissioned by
John Knight
Agency
TBWA Ltd
Client
A.B. Volvo

The artist was asked to illustrate the fable 'The Castle Race'.

Crayon. 60 × 39 cms.

Christopher Wormell

Title
Granary Bap; Wholemeal
Brechan Roll; Milk Loaf
Commissioned by
Gary Walton
Agency
Bartle Bogle Hegarty
Client
St. Ivel

Representations of various
breads with assorted savoury
garnishes were required for St.
Ivel's 'Shape' spread.

Wood engravings.
Each 10 × 8 cms.

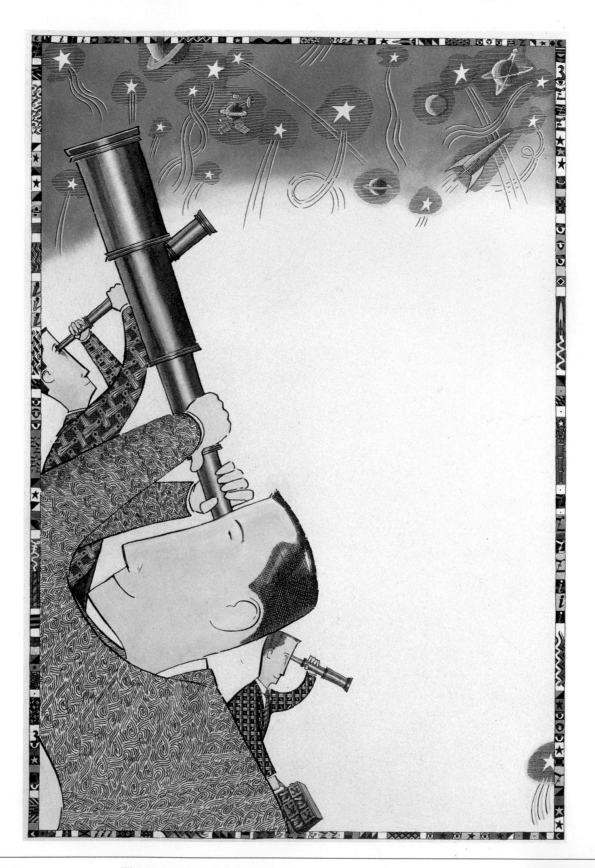

Jeffrey Fisher

Title
Rising Stars
Commissioned by
John Dodson
Agency
Doyle Dane Bernbach Ltd
Client
3i

This is one of a series of press
ads illustrated by the same artist.
The illustration was loosely
based on the art director's rough.

Ink, watercolour. 41 × 27 cms.

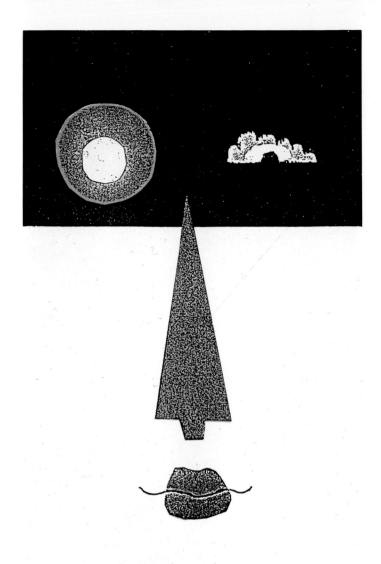

Dolls and Landscapes

AN EXHIBITION OF PAINTINGS BY DAVID LORD

WITH MODEL DOLLS BY MICHAEL LORD

TUESDAY 11 FEBRUARY TO FRIDAY 28 FEBRUARY

LANCASHIRE POLYTECHNIC ARTS CENTRE

ST PETER'S SQUARE FYLDE ROAD PRESTON

10 – 5 MONDAY TO FRIDAY, 10 – 4 SATURDAY

CLOSED 11.30 – 5 TUESDAY 11 FEBRUARY. 12.30 – 2 WEDNESDAY 12 FEBRUARY

Catherine Hicks

Title
Dolls and Landscapes
Commissioned by
Lancashire Polytechnic Arts
Centre

The artist was required to produce a poster for an exhibition which was made up of paintings of dolls set in landscapes and elongated, brightly coloured, papier maché doll heads. The image of a doll, a landscape, and the strange feeling that is induced by looking at dolls had to be conveyed in the poster.

Collage, silkscreen.
59.5 × 25 cms.

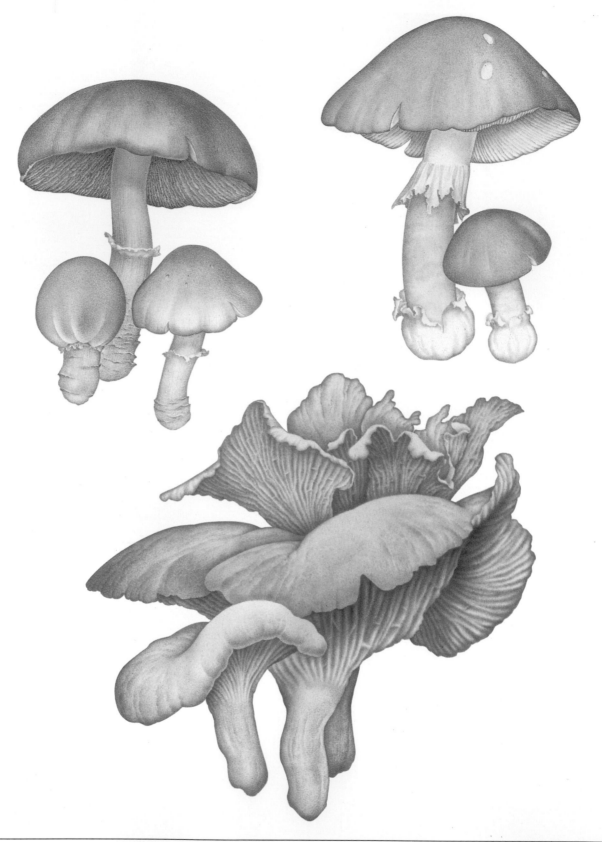

Carol Lawson

Title
How Dangerous is Safe
Advertising?
Commissioned by
Sîan Vickers
Client
Davis Wilkins Advertising Ltd

The illustration was used for the launch of a new design group. The artist's brief was to produce botanically accurate representations of three species of fungi, two harmless culinary varieties and one deadly poisonous; to make the point that advertisers tend to choose advertisements like people choose mushrooms, settling for the bland and safe, rather than risking the less known, but

possibly more rewarding alternatives.

Watercolour. 24 × 18 cms.

Carolyn Gowdy

Title
'Common Ground'—A programme for change in Britain's relations with nature.
Commissioned by
David Holmes
Agency
Holmes Knight Ritchie/WRG Ltd
Client
Common Ground

The artist was asked for an image for a promotional poster for 'Common Ground'. Over the next ten years 'Common Ground' want to bring about a subtle change in the way people think about nature and the land. By encouraging people to value and enjoy their own familiar surroundings, regardless of whether they are rare or unusual, they hope to foster a more self-reliant, less elitist approach to conservation.

Watercolour, inks, collage.
59 × 42 cms.

F8
A
B
C
D

H4

E18
WL

N2

M5

Z
Y
X
W

C42

Tony McSweeney

Title
Beware of the Wolf in Sheep's
Clothing
Commissioned by
Kit Marr, Neil Fazakerley
Agency
Davidson Pearce Ltd
Client
International Wool Secretariat

Continuing the theme of the
current campaign, a convincing
photofit image of a sheep was
required, into which a pair of sly
wolf's eyes was inserted.

Watercolour, pencil, ink.
17 × 14 cms.

David Holmes

Title
The Case Against Caffeine
Commissioned by
Nick Salaman
Client
London Herb & Spice Co.

The artist was asked to illustrate the results of an actual experiment by doctors which discovered that when a remote tribe in Africa was given coffee for the first time they hallucinated. The information is contained in a booklet called 'The Case Against Caffeine' which relates the various disadvantages of drinking too much coffee and tea.

Watercolour. 14 × 10.5 cms.

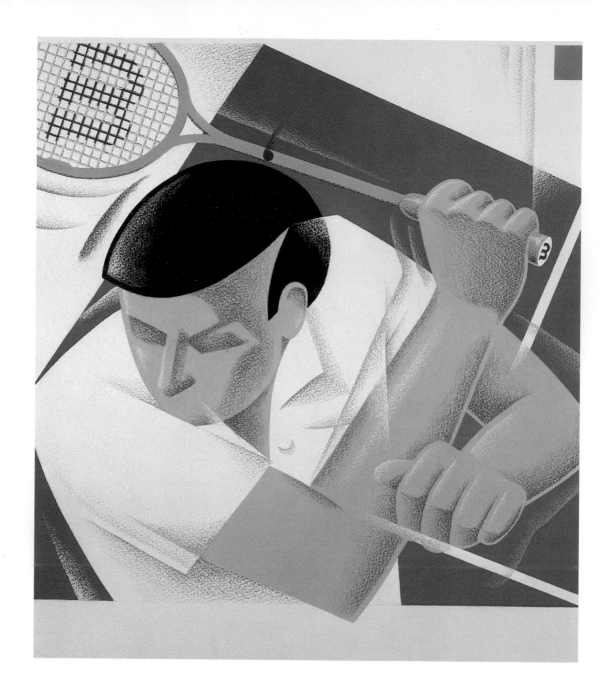

**Bob Norrington,
Peter Tucker**

Title
Wilson Squash Championships
Commissioned by
Viv Thomas
Agency
A. J. Vines & Co
Client
Wilson

The illustration was specifically
required to show the energy of
the game in a stylised graphic
form.

Gouache, pastel. 41 × 41 cms.

**Bob Norrington,
Peter Tucker**

Title
AA Service
Commissioned by
Paul Jarvis
Agency
Fitch & Co.
Client
Automobile Association

This illustration is one in a series
of three frieze panels for the
interior of the AA headquarters
building. The panels had to
cover the range of their services,
this one illlustrates the
breakdown service.

Gouache, pastel. 24 × 60 cms.

David Holmes

Title
Tryst Beneath the Sherry Oak
Commissioned by
David Holmes
Agency
Holmes Knight Ritchie/
WRG Ltd
Client
The Macallan Malt Whisky

The brief was to illustrate the fact that Macallan malt whisky is unique in that it is kept in oaken sherry casks for at least ten years before it is released to meet the bottle.

Ink. 15.5 × 16.5 cms.

BOOK

Paul Cox

Title
The Outing
Commissioned by
Mark Foster, Kathy Miller
Publisher
J. M. Dent & Sons Ltd

The artist was asked to illustrate the book and produce a cover for the short story 'The Outing' by Dylan Thomas. The artist was asked to capture the spirit of a drunken charabanc trip in South Wales, and pay particular attention to the characterisation of the principal figures and to the local architecture; this involved the artist visiting the area in which the book is set.

Watercolour, ink. 70 × 35 cms.

Cathie Felstead

Title
Anya
Commissioned by
Gary Day-Ellison
Publisher
Pan Books Ltd

The artist was given a very tight deadline to produce a portrait of the principal character for the cover of this novel.

Gouache. 40 × 58 cms.

Ingram Pinn

Title
Offensive Marketing
Commissioned by
Steve Kent
Publisher
Penguin Books Ltd

The artist was asked to provide a cover illustration for 'Offensive Marketing', a title in the Penguin Business Library.

Ink, watercolour, crayon.
42 × 36 cms.

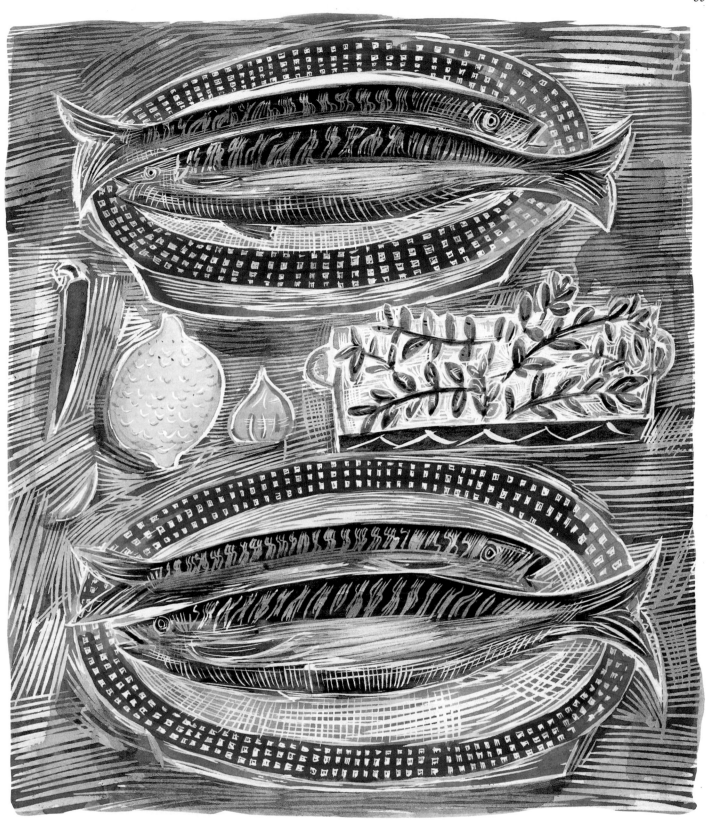

David Sim

Title
Mackerel
Commissioned by
Jim Bunker
Publisher
Walker Books Ltd

This is one of a series of illustrations of classic Italian dishes produced for 'Regional Italian Cooking', one of a set of five cookbooks published for Sainsburys.

Watercolour. 29 × 25 cms.

Richard Adams

Title
Gentlemen of the West
Commissioned by
Steve Kent, David Eldridge
Publisher
Penguin Books Ltd

The book is a humorous romp
set in and around the rough,
tough drinking community of a
lowland Scottish town. The artist
was asked to illustrate the scene
where Proctor Mallion, local slob
and bruiser is physically ejected
from The Paxton Arms.

Chalk pastel. 51.5 × 79 cms

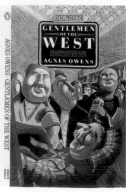

Jean-Christian Knaff

Title
Nights at the Circus
Commissioned by
Gary Day-Ellison
Publisher
Pan Books Ltd

A portrait of the principal
character, Fevvers, was requested
and the cover then left to the
artist's interpretation.

Watercolour, acrylic.
37.5 × 50 cms.

Jonathan Field

Title
Jousting
Commissioned by
Rosie Much
Publisher
P.A. Publishing

This is one of twelve illustrations for a film industry directory, 'The Knowledge'. The artist was given an open brief to illustrate the alphabetical contents page. He chose the letters to illustrate at will and developed his ideas through to finished artwork.

Watercolour. 58 × 38 cms.

Andrew Davidson

Title
The Iron Man
Commissioned by
John McConnell
Publisher
Faber & Faber Ltd

'The Iron Man' was reissued in
two editions, a black and white
version and a deluxe colour
edition. It was felt that carefully
designed, hand coloured wood
engravings would be sympathetic
to the powerful and imaginative
text of Ted Hughes.

Wood engraving, watercolour.
25.5 × 20.5 cms.

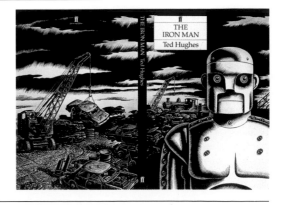

Natacha Ledwidge

Title
Love is Blue
Commissioned by
Claudia Zeff
Publisher
Wm. Heinneman Ltd

The artist was asked to produce cover illustrations for Joan Wyndham's war diaries. For this volume the artist was asked to illustrate the authoress's frequent sense of alienation from the wartime camaraderie surrounding her during her time in the W.A.F.

Charcoal, pastel, crayon.
26 × 18 cms.

Natacha Ledwidge

Title
Love Lessons
Commissioned by
Robin Rout
Publisher
Wm. Heinneman Ltd

The artist was asked to produce cover illustrations for Joan Wyndham's war diaries. This volume is about a teenager's discoveries of men and sex in Bohemian Chelsea during the Second World War.

Charcoal, pastel, crayon.
26 × 18 cms.

Sharon Long

Title
Daddy was a Number Runner
Commissioned by
Ken Leeder
Publisher
Methuen London Ltd

The novel tells the story of a black girl growing up in Harlem during the 1930's. The artist was asked to produce a portrait of the girl; she chose to convey the character's growing realisation of the depressing futility of her approaching adult life in the ghetto.

Pastel. 45 × 72 cms.

Mark Harrison

Title
The Taking of Agnes
Commissioned by
Mark Standley
Publisher
Sphere Books Ltd

An up-market cover with a mysterious and exotic atmosphere was requested for this story set in Martinique, involving the apparent abduction of a beautiful French girl.

Acrylic. 39 × 26 cms.

Ashley Potter

Titles
Spring Sonata, *left*
The Elected Member, *right*
Commissioned by
Liz Laczynska
Publisher
Sphere Books Ltd

These are two in a series of four book covers for novels by Bernice Rubens illustrated by the artist. The artist had to create an overall atmosphere of strangeness and portray the central character in each novel.

Left: This story is told through the consciousness of the unborn baby of a Jewish concert pianist. The baby was a gifted violinist in his previous life who now refuses

to be born and lives inside his mother making music for her alone.

Right: In this book the main character is a 41-year-old barrister who has become a drug addict.

Acrylic. 76.5 × 102 cms.

Ashley Potter

Title
Non-Combatants and Others
Commissioned by
Ken Leeder
Publisher
Methuen & Co Ltd

The artist was asked to produce
an atmospheric illustration for
the book cover. The artist
focuses on the emotions of the
central character, a slightly
crippled artist whose brother dies
in the trenches. The novel is set
in England during the First
World War and so particular
attention had to be paid to the
costumes.

Acrylic. 64 × 96 cms.

Paul Slater

Title
Smallbone Deceased
Commissioned by
Mark Foster
Publisher
J. M. Dent & Sons Ltd

This is the cover illustration for a novel by Michael Gilbert. The illustrator was asked to convey the period of the book and the atmosphere of a 'most respectable' legal firm in which murder has been committed using the classic crime style.

Acrylic. 28.5 × 19 cms.

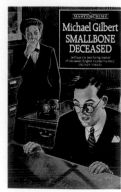

Peter Knock

Title
To Stay Alive
Commissioned by
David Grogan
Publisher
Futura Publications

The artist was given an open brief to illustrate this book cover. The story concerns the plight of a young girl trying to bring up her baby unscathed within a Catholic ghetto in Belfast. The presence of the I.R.A., Protestants and British soldiers are inescapable and her concern is to stay alive both physically and psychologically.

Watercolour. 29 × 17.5 cms.

Sally Davies

Title
The Birth and Death of the
Miracle Man
Commissioned by
Jessica Smith
Publisher
Penguin Books Ltd (Viking
Kestrel imprint)

The artist was asked to illustrate
the central character for this
collection of short stories by
Albert Wendt about his native
Samoa.

Collage. 26 × 33 cms.

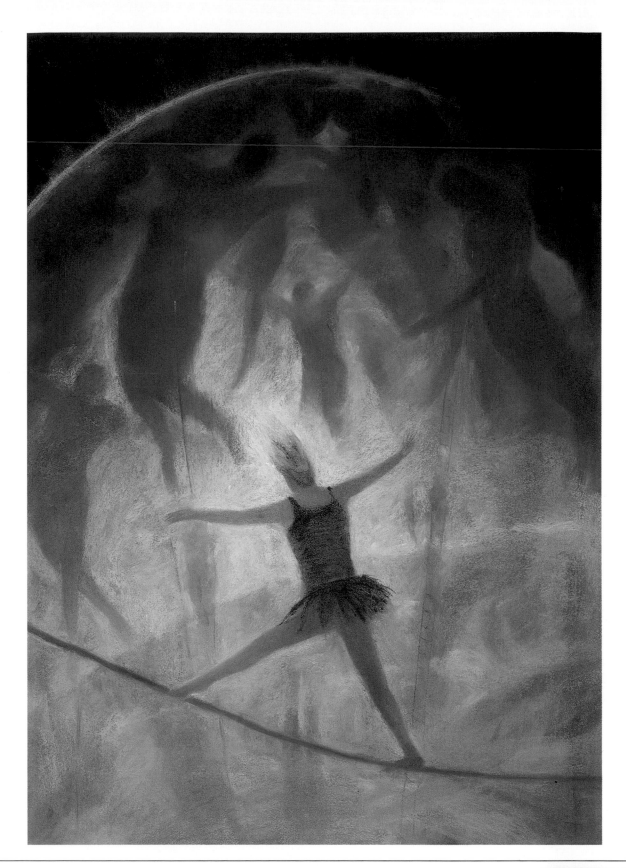

Liz Pyle

Title
Rope Dancer
Commissioned by
Gary Day-Ellison
Publisher
Pan Books Ltd (Picador imprint)

The artist was asked to illustrate the cover of 'Rope Dancer', a collection of short stories by M. J. Fitzgerald.

Pastel. 70 × 100 cms.

Jean-Paul Tibbles

Title
The Great Gatsby
Commissioned by
Steve Kent
Publisher
Penguin Books Ltd

The artist was asked to illustrate the cover of this Penguin Modern Classics title, 'The Great Gatsby' by F. Scott Fitzgerald.

Oil on board. 81 × 50 cms.

Jean-Paul Tibbles

Title
The Pat Hobby Stories
Commissioned by
Steve Kent
Publisher
Penguin Books Ltd

The artist was asked to illustrate the cover of this Penguin Modern Classics title, 'The Pat Hobby Stories' by F. Scott Fitzgerald.

Oil on board. 81 × 50 cms.

Michael Munday

Title
From an Inland Sea
Commissioned by
Steve Kent
Publisher
Penguin Books Ltd

This is the cover illustration for David Harfent's story of a passionate but doomed affair. The drawing had to evoke both the Aegean location and the characters' increasing inability to communicate with each other.

Crayon, oil pastel. 29 × 23 cms.

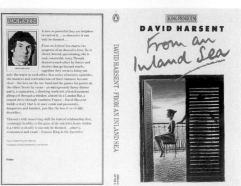

Liz Dalton

Title
Teardrops on my Drum
Commissioned by
Aubrey Walter
Publisher
Gay Men's Press

The artist was asked to depict a scene from the author's childhood in Liverpool in the 1920's where from an early age he was forced to fend for himself.

Acrylic. 76 × 91 cms.

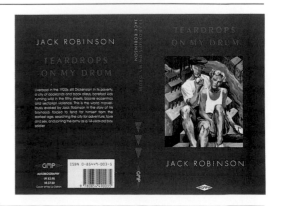

Bill Butcher

Titles
The Last Best Friend, *left*
Inspector Ghote's Good
Crusade, *right*
Not One of Us, *opposite*
Commissioned by
Miles Huddelston
Publisher
Constable & Co. Ltd

Left: The artist was given an open brief to illustrate this crime thriller. What seemed like suicide to everybody else did not seem so the the dead man's best friend.

Watercolour. 22 × 16.5 cms.

Right: The artist was given an open brief to illustrate the cover of this crime thriller set in a Bombay children's refuge. Inspector Ghote is called for when a suspicious death occurs.

Watercolour. 20.5 × 15 cms.

Opposite: The artist was given an open brief to illustrate the cover of this crime thriller set in a village where a girl is murdered. The locals suspect one lonely man but Inspector Finch has other ideas.

Watercolour. 20.5 × 15 cms.

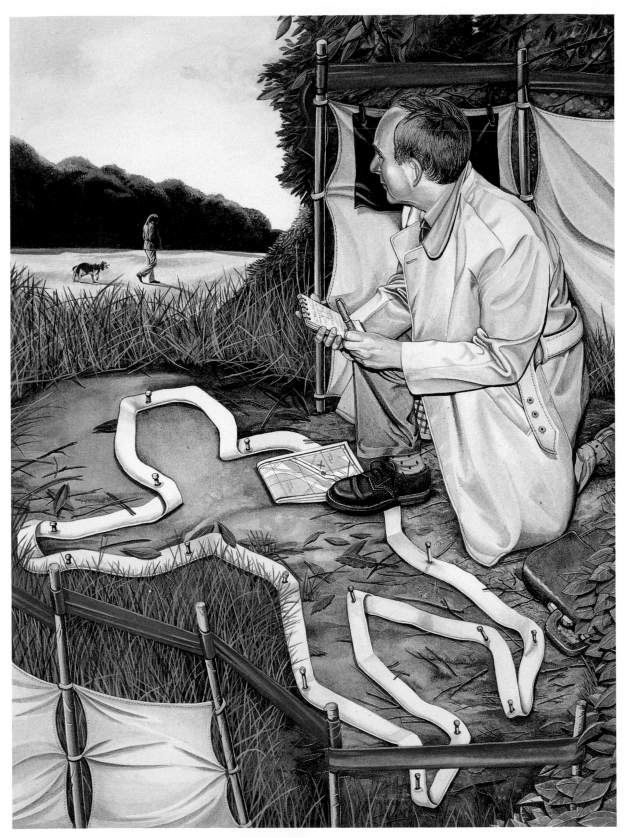

THE LAST BEST FRIEND
George Sims

INSPECTOR GHOTE'S GOOD CRUSADE
H. R. F. Keating

NOT ONE OF US
June Thomson

Martin Handford

Title
Mischief
Commissioned by
Liz Laczynska
Publisher
Sphere Books Ltd

The artist was asked to illustrate
the cover of the Ben Travers
novel, showing the main
characters and events in one
pictorial view.

Pen, watercolour. 23 × 36 cms.

Reg Cartwright

Title
Peter and the Wolf
Commissioned by
Jim Bunker
Publisher
Walker Books Ltd

The illustration is for a book by
Selina Hastings which retells the
classic children's tale of 'Peter
and the Wolf'. The story is based
on the original tale by the
Russian composer Prokofiev.

Oil on board. 51 × 51 cms.

Peter lived with his grandfather in a little house
in the middle of one of the great Russian forests.
The forest was a dark place and during the
winter when the snow lay thickly on the ground,
it could be dangerous. On still nights the
howling of wolves rose clearly into the icy air.
But Peter's home was in a pleasant clearing. It
was surrounded by a garden around which ran a
high stone wall. On the other side of the wall
was a meadow and a pond. Every morning Peter
would come whistling down the path and
through the gate, which he carelessly left open,
his pockets full of bread to feed the duck who
lived on the pond.

Brian Sanders

Title
Leaves from our Tuscan Kitchen
Commissioned by
Steve Kent
Publisher
Penguin Books Ltd

This is the cover illustration for an Italian vegetable cookery book by Janet Ross and Michael Waterford. The artist was asked to provide a landscape evocative of the Tuscan countryside which featured a red roofed farmhouse typical of the area. One third of the illustration had to be left for type.

Watercolour. 41.5 × 26 cms.

Brian Sanders

Title
Wait Until Spring Bandini
Commissioned by
Stephen Abis
Publisher
Grafton Books

The novel by John Fante is about
an Italian immigrant builder
living in Colorado in the 1930's.
The artist was asked for a
painting of the principal
character in his familiar
environment.

Acrylic. 52 × 34.5 cms.

Anne Magill

Title
Main Street
Commissioned by
Steve Kent
Publisher
Penguin Books Ltd

The artist was asked to provide an impressionistic drawing for this book cover. The colours and subject matter had to evoke the atmosphere of a main street of a Western town in the 1800's. The principal characters had to be included on the cover but should not dominate it.

Chalk pastel, acrylic.
74.5 × 122 cms.

Peter Suart

Title
Fontamara
Commissioned by
Kathy Miller
Publisher
J. M. Dent & Sons Ltd

This cover illustration for the novel by Ignazio Silone depicts the young hero, Berardo who represents the defiance of the Fontamara villagers in their tragic struggle against Fascist barbarity.

Oil. 16.5 × 18 cms.

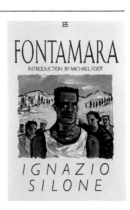

Colin Elgie

Titles
Guide to West Africa, *right*
Guide to Greece, *left*
Commissioned by
Michael Haag
Publisher
Michael Haag

Right: The cover of this guide had to express the tribal elements of West Africa using pattern and texture typical of the region.

Airbrush. 41 × 64.5 cms.

Left: Blue and white were thought to be the colours most suggestive of Greece, being much seen in that country as well as being the colours of the national flag.

Airbrush. 45.5 × 30 cms.

Colin Elgie

Title
Dinosaur & Company
Commissioned by
Steve Kent
Publisher
Penguin Books Ltd

The cover for this book depicts a
number of large corporate
company buildings in the shape
of pre-historic monsters to
suggest that these companies
could soon be a thing of the past.

Airbrush. 28 × 31.5 cms.

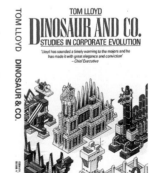

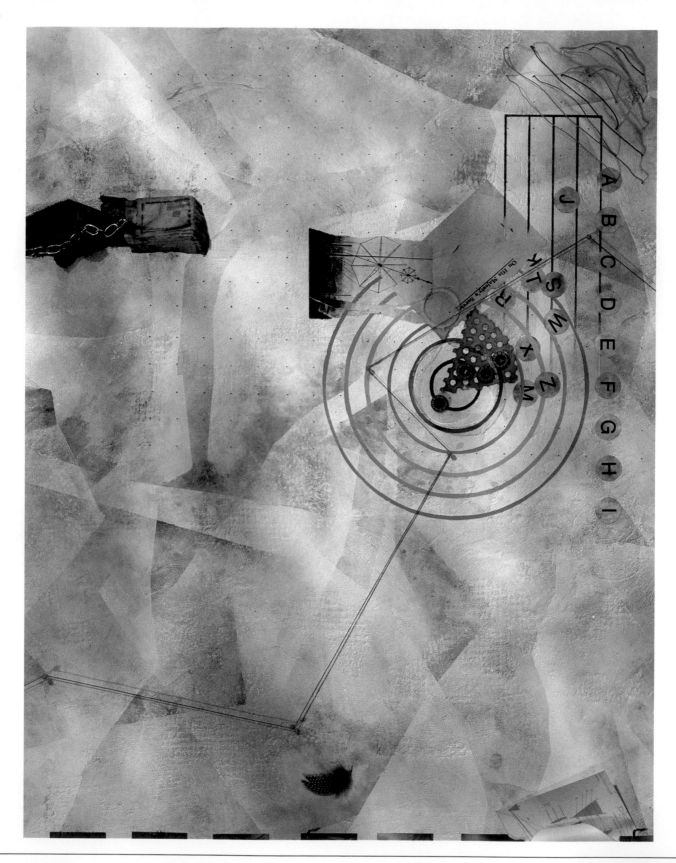

Russell Mills

Title
The Imitation Game
Commissioned by
Gary Day-Ellison
Publisher
Pan Books Ltd (Picador imprint)

The artist was given an open brief to re-design the series of Ian McEwan titles.

Titles opposite page
The Cement Garden, *above left*
In Between the Sheets, *above right*
First Love, Last Rites, *below left*
The Comfort of Strangers, *below right*

Details from mixed media construction.
122 × 122 × 6 cms.

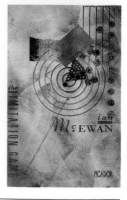

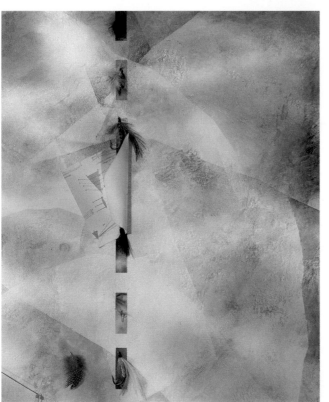

Nick Hardcastle

Titles
That Yew Tree's Shade, *left*
Death is No Sportsman, *right*
Tragedy at Law, *opposite*
Commissioned by
Ian Chilvers at Faber & Faber
and
Marcus Hewitt at Pentagram
Design
Publisher
Faber & Faber Ltd

The artist was given the covers of a series of murder mystery books by Cyril Hare to illustrate. He had to do so in a dramatic manner, conveying the period of the 1920's and 30's in which the books are set.

Left: In this instance the majority of the story is based on the events in a small, provincial English town and the artist wanted to suggest the mysterious murder of a woman from this environment.

Right: This particular story is about a group of men who take a Summer fishing trip and subsequently discover a mysterious murder.

Pen and ink. 16.5 × 26.5 cms.

Opposite: For this title the artist felt it important to show that most of the story is set in the law courts and to convey the sinister aspects of the book.

Pen and ink. 16.5 × 26.5 cms.

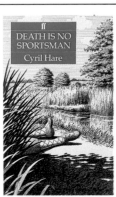

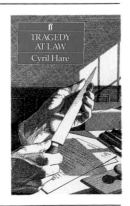

Anne Yvonne Gilbert

Title
Christmas Day
Commissioned by
Michael Mendelsohn
Publisher
The Franklin Library

A silhouette image was required for a limited edition book, 'The Sketchbook of Geoffrey Crayon, Gent' by Washington Irving.

Pen and ink. 10 × 18 cms.

The Sketch Book
of
Geoffrey Crayon, Gent.

Anne Yvonne Gilbert

Title
Geoffrey Crayon
Commissioned by
Michael Mendelsohn
Publisher
The Franklin Library

A silhouette of the character of
the title was required for a
limited edition book, 'The
Sketchbook of Geoffrey Crayon,
Gent' by Washington Irving.

Pen and ink. 7 × 8 cms.

Michael Cole

Titles
Above: A Christmas Carol—
Fezziwig's Ball
Below: Street Scene with Scrooge
and Third Ghost
Commissioned by
Michael Cole
Publisher
Pagoda Books

This entirely new edition of 'A
Christmas Carol' is the
culmination of the artist's
personal ambition to illustrate
Dickens' classic tale. The book
was produced in strip format
with balloons for the dialogue
(hand-written, as with political
cartoons of the time), whilst
suitable typography was used for
the narrative. John Leech's
original plates suggested the style

to be used since the artist's aim
was to evoke the period and to
remain true to Dickens' text.

Line and watercolour ink.
52 × 25 cms.

Ralph Steadman

Title
In the Underworld
Commissioned by
Nick Murphy
Publisher
Allen & Unwin Publishers Ltd

The artist was asked to convey
the atmosphere and chilling
nature of the full-time
professional villain's underworld
existence as revealed by the
author Laurie Taylor.

Inks. 55 × 48 cms.

Alastair Taylor

Title
Losing Control
Commissioned by
Lorraine Owen
Publishers
Macdonald & Co. (Publishers)
Ltd

This cover illustration is for a
novel by Shirley Lowe and
Angela Ince about a media
woman whose world crumbles
about her when it becomes
apparent that her seemingly
perfect life is maintained by her
ruthless exploitation of her
friends and colleagues.

Pencil, watercolour.
18 × 11 cms.

Sally Lecky-Thompson

Title
Gentleman and Players
Commissioned by
Lorraine Owen
Publisher
Futura Publications

This book is a sequel to 'Privileged Children'. For this reason the brief had two main points; the cover had to be treated in the same way as the previous book and incorporate a decorative panel for the type and secondly the main characters had to be shown with the emphasis on the women as 'players'.

Gouache. 18 × 11 cms.

Barbara Lofthouse

Title
Birds of Paradise
Commissioned by
Steve Abis
Publisher
Wm. Collins & Sons & Co Ltd

A series of book covers for novels
by Paul Scott were illustrated
using landscape as a unifying
theme. This story is set on a
Pacific island.

Gouache. 28.5 × 46 cms.

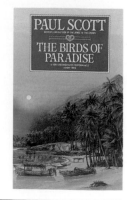

Graham Rawle

Title
August in July
Commissioned by
Michael Brown
Publisher
Hamish Hamilton Ltd

This illustration is for the cover of Carlo Gébler's second novel. By recording his thoughts in a notebook, August Slemic attempts to free himself from the prison of loneliness.

Collage. 27.5 × 18 cms.

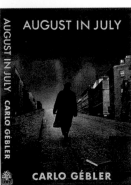

Janet Woolley

Title
Stunning the Punters
Commissioned by
Hugh Adams
Publisher
Faber & Faber Ltd

The artist was asked to illustrate
the title story in a collection of
short stories by Robert Sproat.

Acrylic. 54 × 35 cms.

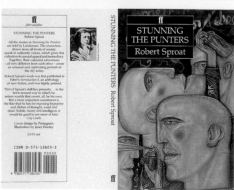

Catherine Denvir

Title
A Certain Smile
Commissioned by
Steve Kent, Eddie Edwards
Publisher
Penguin Books Ltd

The artist was asked to illustrate
this book cover for a Françoise
Sagan novel in her own
particular style.

Collage, watercolour.
30 × 20.5 cms.

EDITORIAL

Ian Pollock

Title
Elemental Effluvia
Commissioned by
Roger Watt
Publication
Men Only
Company
Paul Raymond Publications Ltd

The artist was asked to illustrate the do's and don'ts of a gentleman's reek.

Watercolour, ink, gouache.
55 × 44 cms.

AWARD

CREATIVE REVIEW

This illustration has been selected to receive the 1986 Creative Review Award for the Best Use of Humour.

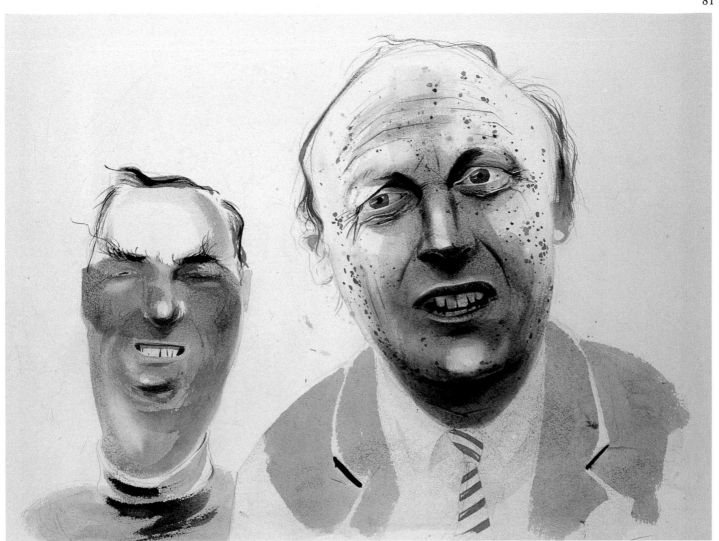

Ian Pollock

Title
Cabinet Pudding: Denis Healey
and Neil Kinnock
Commissioned by
John Tennant
Publication
The Observer Colour Magazine
Company
The Observer

These are two of seventeen
political portraits which
accompanied a speculation on
what might happen if Labour
won the next General Election,
but without gaining an overall
majority. Mr Kinnock would be
forced to seek a power-sharing
deal with the Alliance.

Watercolour, ink. gouache.
44 × 55 cms.

Robin Harris

Title
Der Angeleitete Chef
Commissioned by
Dr Peter Derschka
Publication
Management Wissen
Company
Vogel Verlag

The artist was asked for an illustration after receiving a phone call saying, "The article is about junior management manipulating their bosses, can you do something?"

Acrylic, pastel. 50.5 × 59.5 cms.

Robin Harris

Title
Case No.38
Commissioned by
Iris Lynch
Publication
Mims Magazine
Company
Medical Publications Ltd

The artist was asked to illustrate the following text, "An 18-year-old student has one child; last year, had one termination for an unwanted pregnancy; she comes to the doctor fearing that she has become pregnant again, and wishes the doctor to do something."

Acrylic, pastel. 37 × 52 cms.

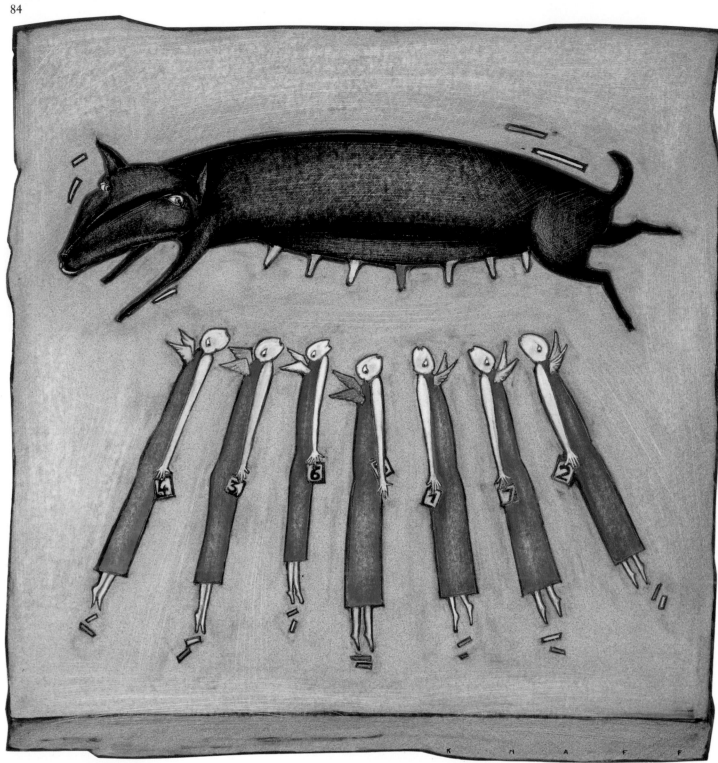

Jean-Christian Knaff

Title
Groups of Seven
Commissioned by
Chris Jones
Publication
New Scientist
Company
IPC Magazines Ltd

The artist was asked to produce
an illustration for the cover story
about how things seem to work in
groups of seven.

Watercolour, coloured pencil.
31 × 33 cms.

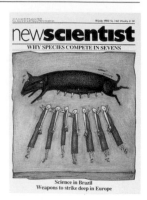

Warren Madill

Title
Rajiv Ghandi
Commissioned by
Pedro Silmon
Publication
Sunday Times Magazine
Company
The Sunday Times

A strong portrait of the Indian
Prime Minister, Rajiv Ghandi
was required. The portrait is
executed in the style of the
traditional 18th and 19th century
Indian painters. The object was
to portray Rajiv Ghandi as a man
with an eye to the future, hence
he wears a digital watch and
modern buildings and aeroplanes
are arranged decoratively in the
background.

Acrylic. 52.5 × 43 cms.

Peter Knock

Title
Talked to Death
Commissioned by
Derek Ungless
Publication
Rolling Stone
Company
Straight Arrow Publishers Inc.

The artist was asked to recreate actual events in the life of abusive, American, radio phone-in D.J., Alan Berg. He was shot dead whilst leaving his car, by an outraged listener. It was decided to use the composition in a symbolic manner to heighten the idea of complete role reversal.

Watercolour. Each 21 × 21 cms.

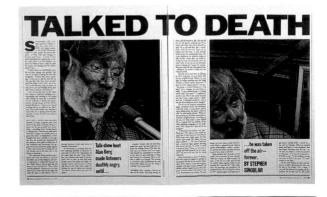

TALKED TO DEATH

Talk-show host Alan Berg made listeners deathly angry, until...

...he was taken off the air— forever.

BY STEPHEN SINGULAR

James Marsh

Title
Endangered Species
Commissioned by
Mike Lackersteen
Publication
Airport Magazine
Company
Redwood Publishing Ltd

The artist was asked to produce an illustration for a feature about endangered species, particularly those threatened with extinction due to the tourist trade.

Acrylic on canvas board.
50 × 40 cms.

Catherine Denvir

Title
Carnivorous Man Now
Cultivates His Garden
Commissioned by
John Bradley
Publication
The Listener
Company
BBC Publications

The illustration accompanied an
article about the growing
influence of vegetarianism.

Watercolour, collage.
23 × 29 cms.

Christopher Wormell

Title
Birdwatch
Commissioned by
Tim Walmsley
Publication
Radio Times
Company
BBC Publications

An illustration was required for a 'Birdwatch' programme, broadcast live from the Wildfoul Trust at Martin Mere. The artist was asked to show pink foot geese which arrive at the Trust in large numbers to take refuge from the Arctic winter.

Woodcut. 12 × 11 cms.

Trevor Boyer

Title
Swallows, Swifts, House Martins
and Sand Martins
Commissioned by
Pedro Silmon
Publication
Sunday Times Magazine
Company
The Sunday Times

The artist was asked to illustrate
swallows, swifts, house martins
and sand martins in one dramatic
image.

Watercolour, gouache.
37 × 31.5 cms.

Emma Chichester Clark

Title
Knoxville 'Summer of 1915'
Commissioned by
Jenny Fleet
Publication
Radio Times
Company
BBC Publications

The artist was asked to depict an autobiographical dream sequence from James Agee's childhood, set to music by Samuel Barber.

Pencil, ink. 19 × 31 cms.

Grahame Baker

Title
The Conversation
Commissioned by
Wendy Varley
Publication
Just Seventeen
Company
EMAP

The illustration accompanied a short story about a girl who works in the household plants department of a large store. The girl holds fantasy conversations with one of her customers.

Acrylic, household emulsion, crayon. 28 × 24 cms.

Janet Woolley

Title
In Search of a Novel
Commissioned by
Tacye Davis
Publication
Expression!
Company
Redwood Publishing Ltd

An illustration was required to accompany a travel diary in which the author Leslie Thomas traces the journey the characters of his new novel are destined to take.

Acrylic, crayon. 38 × 29.5 cms.

Janet Woolley

Title
I Claudius
Commissioned by
Jane Bogue
Publication
Radio Times
Company
BBC Publications

An illustration was needed for a radio drama about Tiberius Claudius. The artist was asked to illustrate the last scene of the play. In the wake of the mayhem following Caligula's assassination, Claudius, reluctantly on his part, is proclaimed emperor.

Pencil. 25 × 18 cms.

Carolyn Gowdy

Title
For Good or Evil
Commissioned by
Martin Colyer
Publication
The Listener
Company
BBC Publications

This is an illustration for a short story by Clive Sinclair. "He buried me prematurely in the cold ground, without a word of comfort or advice, as though he expected me to know in advance how to escape. Certainly my instinct was to do just that, but it was an uneducated instinct, clueless as to how to translate desire into action."

Watercolour, ink, collage.
67 × 193 cms.

Ducking out

The directions were explicit. We were to take
the route national towards Cahors, turn off
at the D29, pass under the autoroute and bear
sharp left when we saw the duck.

Carolyn Gowdy

Title
Ducking Out
Commissioned by
Shem Law
Publication
The Observer Colour Magazine
Company
The Observer

The illustration was
commissioned for the Sue Arnold
page of the supplement. While
on a journey in France, Sue
Arnold together with the winner
of the Observer Truffle
Competition and his family are
invited to witness the ancient and
controversial custom of force-
feeding geese to produce foie
gras.

Watercolour, ink. 65 × 77 cms.

Matt Mahurin

Title
Machiavellian Management
Commissioned by
Mike Lackersteen
Publication
Venture U.K.
Company
Redwood Publishing Ltd

An illustration was required to accompany an article which examined the parallel between modern management techniques and the statecraft described in the 15th century book, 'The Prince' by Machiavelli.

Oil. 24 × 17 cms.

Ellis Nadler

Title
Western Drugs Shower the
Third World
Commissioned by
John Bradley
Publication
The Listener
Company
BBC Publications

The artist was asked to illustrate
the cover story about the
dangerous practice of some
Western companies who
distribute drugs to the Third
World which have not been
properly tested, or have been
rejected by the West.

Gouache. 21.5 × 18 cms.

THE LISTENER

Western drugs shower the Third World
Ken Vass
Norman Buchan Peacock's 'Rambo remit'
Stuart Simon, John Simpson Spy tales
Tom Mangold Privatising the prisons

Christopher Corr

Title
Star Wars: The Computer
Strikes Back
Commissioned by
Peter Green
Publication
Personal Computer World
Company
VNU Business Publications

The artist was asked to illustrate
an article about the use of
computers in the Star Wars
conflict.

Collage, ink, gouache.
70 × 50 cms.

Robin Harris

Title
At the Heart of the Killing
Machine
Commissioned by
Pedro Silmon, Mike Rand
Publication
Sunday Times Magazine
Company
The Sunday Times

The artist was asked to produce a
one and a half page spread to
accompany an article about
soldiers' experiences in the army.

Acrylic, pastel. 73 × 47.5 cms.

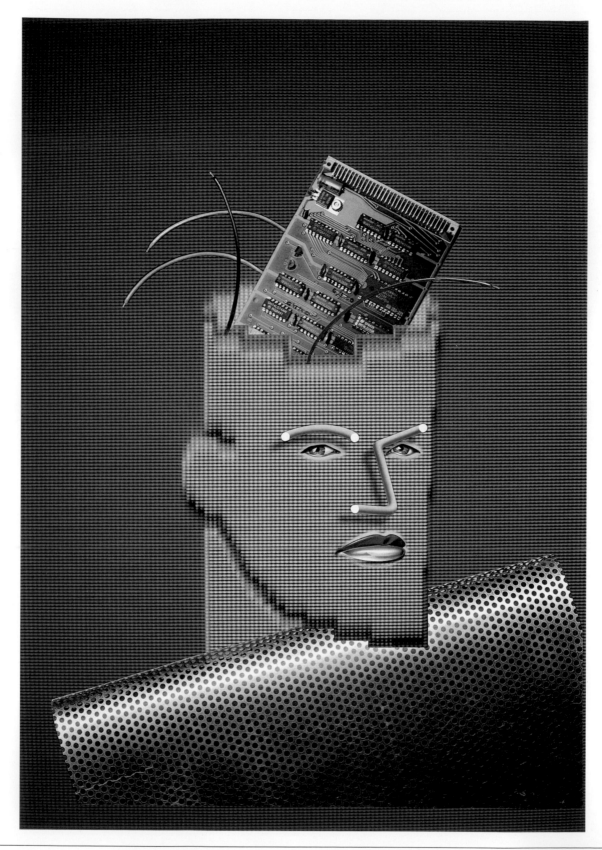

Paul Allen

Title
Memory Expansion
Commissioned by
Mike Spiller
Publication
Computing Age
Company
EMAP

The illustration was commissioned for the cover of 'Computing Age' and was based on the feature article about memory expansion modules which increase the power of existing computers. 'Computer Age' magazine was discontinued and the illustration appeared on the cover of 'I C Designer Supplement' in 'Cadcam International' magazine.

Photo-montage, computer graphics, airbrush. 45 × 33 cms.

Paul Allen

Title
Artificial Intelligence
Commissioned by
Mike Spiller
Publication
Q L User
Company
EMAP

This is one of a series of illustrations on the theme of artificial intelligence. The illustration accompanied an article which used a thunder storm to illustrate one of the points in the article.

Photo-montage, computer graphics, airbrush. 43 × 30 cms.

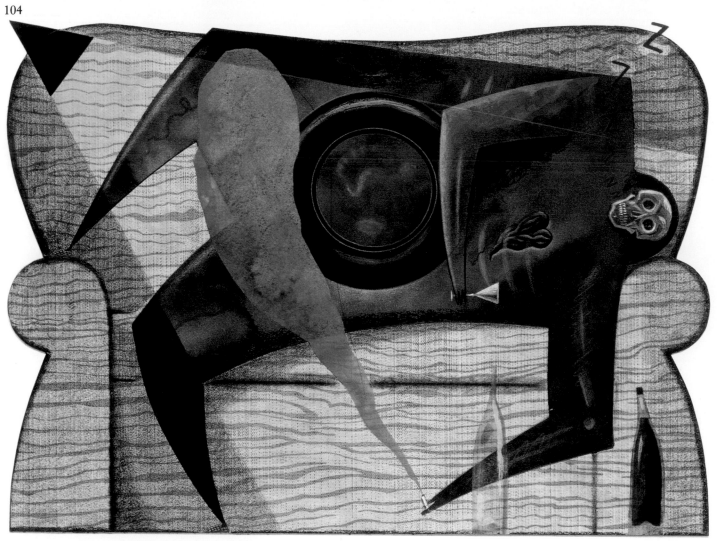

Robert Mason

Title
Why Exercise is Good for the
Brain
Commissioned by
Jim Brewster
Publication
Inter-City Magazine
Company
Redwood Publishing Ltd

The illustration accompanied an
article on health care for
executives.

Gouache. 14.5 × 20.5 cms.

Andrzej Dudzinski

Title
Elle Horoscope
Commissioned by
Clive Crook, Malgosia Szemberg
Publication
Elle
Company
News International Hachette

The artist was given an open brief to interpret the starsign Sagittarius.

Watercolour. 5 × 18 cms.

Lynda Gray

Title
'Vogue' cover
Commissioned by
Clare White
Publication
Creative Review
Company
Centaur Communications Ltd

The article argued that certain magazines, including 'Vogue', were not using illustration to its fullest extent. Several artists were commissioned to show how illustration could be used on their covers.

Gouache. 33 × 25 cms.

Paul Slater

Title
Artists and Models
Commissioned by
Jenny Fleet
Publication
Radio Times
Company
BBC Publications

An illustration was required for a dramatised television series about three revolutionary French artists and their relationships, both private and public, with their models.

Acrylic. 26 × 34.5 cms.

Richard Draper

Title
RAC Rally
Commissioned by
Jenny Fleet
Publication
Radio Times
Company
BBC Publications

The artist ws asked to produce an illustrative map of the RAC rally course through Great Britain.

Gouache, ink. 38.5 × 33 cms.

David Suter

Title
The Proms—American Style
Commissioned by
Martin Colyer
Publication
The Listener
Company
BBC Publications

The artist was asked for a cover
illustration related to the feature
article about the American
composer, Roger Sessions. Roger
Sessions died earlier in the year
and his last opera received its
European premier at the Proms
in the week covered by this issue
of 'The Listener'.

Coloured pencil. 40 × 34 cms.

David Sim

Title
Fishy Starters
Commissioned by
Clive Crook
Publication
The Observer Colour Magazine
Company
The Observer

The artist was asked to produce
an illustration to show some of
the starter dishes that could be
made using seafood.

Watercolour. 30 × 25 cms.

David Sim

Title
The Berry Idea
Commissioned by
Joy Hannington
Publication
Homes and Gardens
Company
IPC Magazines Ltd

The artist was asked to produce an illustration which showed dishes that could be made using fresh-grown berries.

Watercolour. 37 × 27 cms.

Peter Till

Title
Bottle and Glasses
Commissioned by
Jim Brewster
Publication
Intercity
Company
Redwood Publishing Ltd

The artist was asked for an
illustration to accompany an
article about incipient alcoholism
among businessmen who think
that they are only drinking
socially.

Watercolour, pen and ink.
22 × 32 cms.

Peter Till

Title
Lunch on You
Commissioned by
Mike Lackersteen
Publication
Airport Magazine
Company
Redwood Publishing Ltd

The artist was asked to illustrate
a feature on the art of the
business lunch.

Watercolour, pen and ink.
33 × 27 cms.

Peter Till

Title
Channel Tunnel
Commissioned by
John Bradley
Publication
Spectator
Company
John Fairfax Ltd

The artist was asked for an illustration to accompany an article about the respective benefits and drawbacks of a channel tunnel linking Britain and France.

Watercolour, pen and ink.
38 × 27 cms.

Mick Brownfield

Title
Politicians at Play
Commissioned by
Elizabeth Thompson
Publication
Airport Magazine
Company
Redwood Publishing Ltd

The artist was asked to illustrate a feature on how politicians, so often recognised in public, find it difficult to take a quiet holiday.

Airbrush. 34.5 × 25 cms.

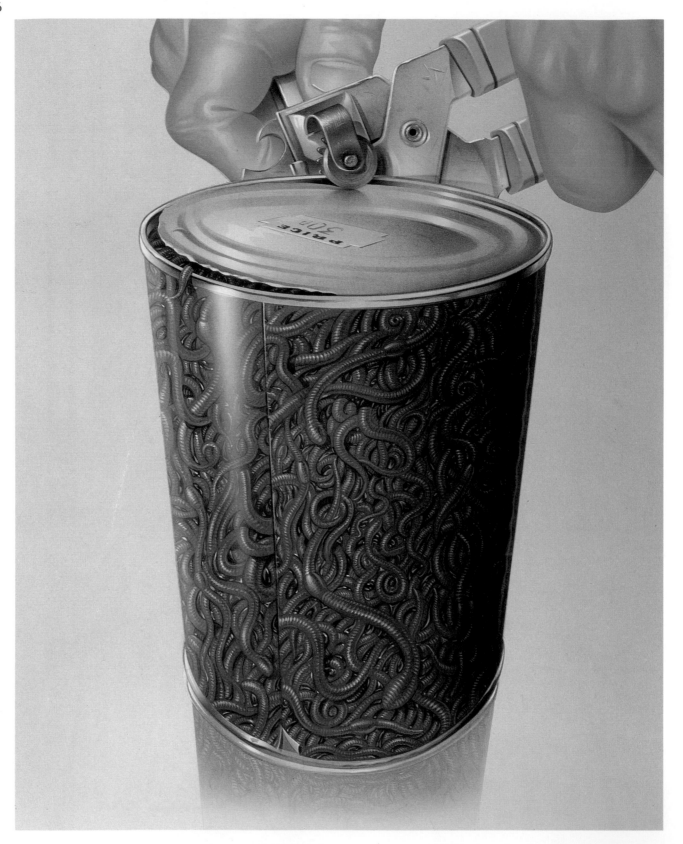

Mick Brownfield

Title
Food Additives/Can of Worms
Commissioned by
Pedro Silmon
Publication
Sunday Times Magazine
Company
The Sunday Times

The illustration was originally commissioned as a striking cover image to introduce the first of a series of features on food additives. The resulting illustration was judged to be a little strong for the Sunday breakfast table and was used inside the magazine instead.

Airbrush. 32 × 40 cms.

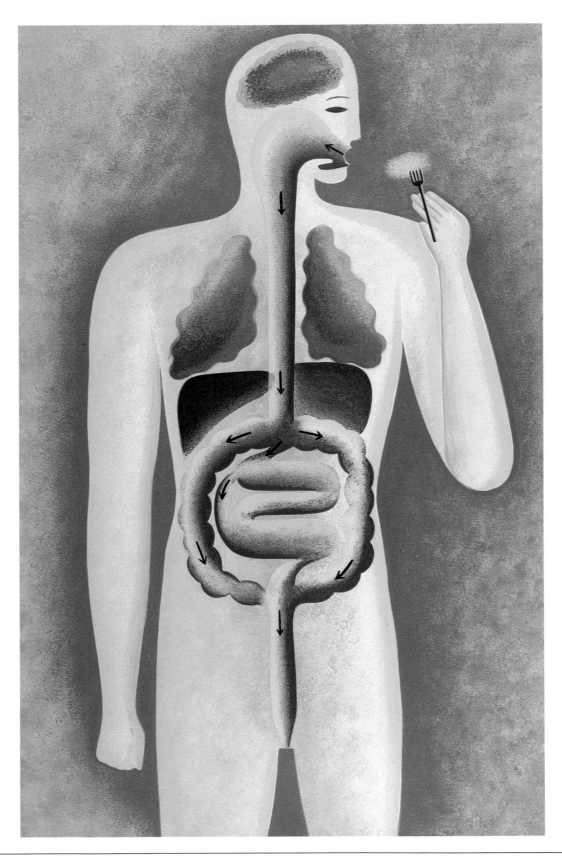

Paul Leith

Title
Food Additives
Commissioned by
Pedro Silmon
Publication
Sunday Times Magazine
Company
The Sunday Times

The artist was asked to illustrate
the system of investigating food
additives in the U.K. using the
human body in a diagramatical
way.

Acrylic. 33.5 × 46.5 cms.

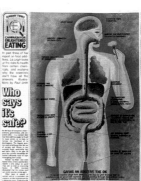

Richard Parent

Title
Techno Fear
Commissioned by
Theo Hodges
Publication
The Decision Maker
Company
Rank Xerox

The artist was asked to illustrate
the fear of new technology from
an historical point of view.
"Consciously or subconsciously,
many people feel that the
machine kills the personal self;
brings material gain but spiritual,
moral and imaginative loss;
destroys natural body rhythm;
separates man from nature."

Oil pastel, gouache, collage.
21 × 30 cms.

Ian Beck

Title
Summer Holidays
Commissioned by
Brian Thomas
Publication
Radio Times
Company
BBC Publications

The artist was asked for a cover illustration for a supplement to the Radio Times about holiday travel.

Watercolour, coloured pencils.
24 × 31 cms.

Brian Grimwood

Title
French Style
Commissioned by
Janetta Lewin
Publication
The Observer Colour Magazine
Company
The Observer

The artist was asked for an illustration to evoke French style for the 'Living Extra' supplement. He chose to represent many various elements associated with French culture.

Gouache. 42 × 48 cms.

Jim Mawtus

Title
Da Doo Rom Rom
Commissioned by
Mike Lackersteen
Publication
Acorn User
Company
Redwood Publishing Ltd

The artist was asked to illustrate
an article on the many
accessories available to computer
owners.

Watercolour, ink. 29.5 × 28 cms.

George Hardie

Title
Harvey Nichols
Commissioned by
Richard Krzyzak
Publication
Harpers & Queen
Company
National Magazine Company

The artist was asked to produce a decorative map of Harvey Nichols for a special issue of Harpers.

Ink, crayon. 60 × 39.5 cms.

Bush Hollyhead

Title
Jazz Week
Commissioned by
Jenny Fleet
Publication
Radio Times
Company
BBC Publications

The artist was asked to provide the cover illustration for an issue reviewing a series of programmes on jazz.

Gouache, ink. 32 × 39 cms.

Jeffrey Fisher

Title
Fluffy
Commissioned by
John Tennant
Publication
Sunday Times Magazine
Company
The Sunday Times

The artist was given an open
brief to illustrate an article about
wine tasting kits.

Watercolour. 36 × 15 cms.

Jeffrey Fisher

Title
Hangover
Commissioned by
Tacye Davis
Publication
Expression!
Company
Redwood Publishing Ltd

The artist was given an open
brief to illustrate an article about
hangovers.

Watercolour. 27 × 18 cms.

Edward Briant

Title
The Lost Cottage
Commissioned by
Steven Stafford
Publication
Womans Journal
Company
IPC Magazines Ltd

The artist was asked to produce
an illustration for a short story
set in an old fishing village in
Cape Cod, Massachusetts.
Whilst on holiday with his
family, a young New Yorker has
his first sexual experience with a
fisherman.

Gouache. 30 × 30 cms.

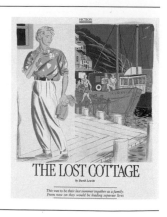

Sue Dray

Title
Talking Dirty
Commissioned by
Glynn Platz
Publication
Gay Times

The illustration was to accompany an article on the ever expanding business of telephone obscenity which originated in America and has now been popularised in this country.

Pencil. 35 × 31.5 cms.

Chris Priestley

Title
Tom Waits
Commissioned by
Mike Pilgrim
Publication
R.M.
Company
Spotlight Publications

The artist was asked for a caricature of Tom Waits for the letters page of R.M. magazine.

Pen and ink. 35 × 30 cms.

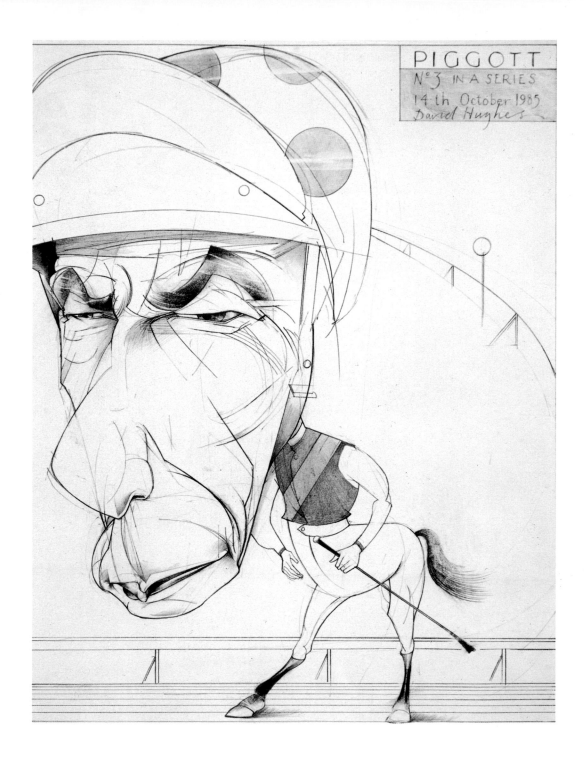

David Hughes

Title
Lester Piggott
Commissioned by
Tim Walmsley
Publication
Radio Times
Company
BBC Publications

A caricature of Lester Piggott was required to illustrate a programme which profiled his career.

Pencil. 26.5 × 20.5 cms.

FRIDAY TV 1 November
BBC 1
BBC 2
THE WEEKEND STARTS HERE

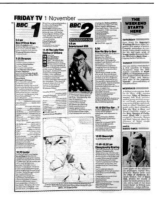

Chris Burke

Title
Ireland Through Irish Eyes
Commissioned by
John Bradley
Publication
The Listener
Company
BBC Publications

The artist was asked to illustrate
a special issue covering various
Irish topics with articles by
several Irish writers.

Watercolour, pen and ink.
43 × 55 cms.

THE LISTENER

Ireland through Irish eyes
*J.J. Lee, Padraig Yeates, Dick Walsh,
Emily O'Reilly, Peter Lennon, Homan
Potterton, Mary Kenny's Diary*
Bel Mooney How I was wronged by the Mirror

Tony Watson

Title
British Sherry
Commissioned by
Pedro Silmon
Publication
Sunday Times Magazine
Company
The Sunday Times

The artist was asked for an
illustration to accompany an
article which lamented the fact
that certain British sherry
companies had fought off
Spanish protests, and were being
allowed to use the term 'sherry'
for their own inferior products.

Watercolour, pen and ink.
20 × 18 cms.

Peter Morter

Title
Woodland Trees
Commissioned by
John Tenant
Publication
Sunday Times Magazine
Company
The Sunday Times

The artist was asked to produce seven illustrations of trees and their fruit selected from the article, 'Fight to Save the Greenwood'.

Watercolour, pen and ink.
31 × 25 cms.

Peter Morter

Title
Traditional Fruits
Commissioned by
John Tennant
Publication
Sunday Times Magazine
Company
The Sunday Times

The artist was asked for a selection of fruits to illustrate an article called 'Fruits of his Labour'.

Watercolour, pen and ink.
36 × 28 cms.

Peter Morter

Title
Kingston Lacy, Dorset
Commissioned by
Clive Crook
Publication
The Observer Colour Magazine
Company
The Observer

The artist was asked for a cut-away illustration showing the interior of Kingston Lacy for an article on the restoration of buildings and the work of The National Trust.

Watercolour, pen and ink.
44 × 38 cms.

PRINT AND DESIGN

Print and Design Judging Panel
Mary Lewis, designer, Lewis Moberly;
Andrew McNab, illustrator; Neil Smith,
designer, Lloyd Northover; Bruno Tilley,
Creative Director, Island Records;
Christopher Wormell, illustrator.

Christopher Brown

Title
Toots and the Maytals
Commissioned by
Bruno Tilley
Design Group
Island Art
Client
Island Records

The art director felt that the artist's work reflected the mood of the music. An illustration was required that showed Toots as one of the founder members of the reggae movement, teaching his followers.

Lino cut. 48 × 48 cms.

Cathie Felstead

Title
Jimmy Cliff
Commissioned by
Bruno Tilley
Design Group
Island Art
Client
Island Records

The artist was asked to capture something of the sharp gangster character which Jimmy Cliff portrayed in the film 'The Harder They Come', and to show him in a vibrant downtown setting.

Pastel. 43 × 43 cms.

Sue Curtis

Title
Angel Maimone 'Ultimo Ballo'
('The Last Dance')
Commissioned by
Bruno Tilley
Design Group
Island Art
Client
Island Records

The artist was asked to produce a
theatrical image which reflects
the romantic theme of 'The Last
Dance'. She was asked to use a
few specific colours and to
feature pictures of the band
within the illustration.

Mixed media. 61 × 61 cms.

Sue Curtis

Title
Strictly for Lovers
Commissioned by
Bruno Tilley
Design Group
Island Art
Client
Island Records

The artist was asked to illustrate this compilation album. She had to feature two lovers in an abstract style and incorporate symbolic references to the Rastafarian religion.

Pen and ink. 48 × 48 cms.

Paul Leith

Title
Third World 'Now that We've Found Love'
Commissioned by
Bruno Tilley
Design Group
Island Art
Client
Island Records

The artist was asked to produce a simple, figurative illustration showing two lovers dancing on a sunlit tropical beach, conveying the light, optimistic feel of the song.

Acrylic. 43 × 43 cms.

Ian Pollock

Title
Black Uhuru
Commissioned by
Bruno Tilley
Design Group
Island Art
Client
Island Records

The artist was asked to show
Black Uhuru as a hard
uncompromising reggae band.

Watercolour, ink, gouache.
53 × 53 cms.

The Chocolate Salesboy. Pollock 85

Ian Pollock

Title
The Chocolate Salesboy
Commissioned by
Jill George
Design Group
Thumb Design
Client
Thumb Gallery

The artist was asked for an image
for use in the Thumb Gallery
calendar 1986.

Watercolour, ink, gouache.
55 × 37 cms.

Ingram Pinn

Title
Tailored Systems
Commissioned by
Jim Allen
Design Group
Jim Allen Design Group
Client
Norton Telecommunications

The artist was asked to illustrate
the ability of the client to design
telecommunications systems to
suit a variety of customers.

Ink, crayon. 38 × 30 cms.

Gary Wing

Title
An Unjust U.S. Tax Exposed
Commissioned by
Shawen Haymen
Design Group
Lloyd Northover Ltd
Client
B.A.T. Industries PLC

This brochure illustration
accompanied an article about the
ways in which the U.S. tax
department was unfairly taxing
many industries in Britain and
other countries. The illustration
had to depict the main street of a
small town where dollar bills are
being sucked into the tax
department.

Watercolour, ink. 41 × 33 cms.

Catherine Denvir

Title
Scenes from an Execution
Commissioned by
Jill Hiley
Design Group
BBC Information Design
Department
Client
BBC Publications

The artist was asked to produce a cover illustration for a brochure for a BBC radio drama entry for the Italia Prize 1985. The play is about a woman painter who has been commissioned by the Doge to paint a scene from the Venetian sea battle of Le Panto.

Collage, watercolour.
30 × 20 cms.

Liz Pyle

Title
Fine Wine
Commissioned by
David Riches, David Brennan
Design Group
Fitch & Co
Client
Roberts & Cooper Wine
Merchants

The artist was asked to illustrate
a small poster for the fine wines
section of Roberts & Cooper
Wine Merchants.

Pastel. 70 × 100 cms.

Jane Human

Title
H. Allen Smith
Commissioned by
Mary Lewis
Design Group
Lewis Moberly
Client
H. Allen Smith

The artist was asked to create a logo for this wine merchant.

Oil on canvas. 50 × 61 cms.

George Hardie

Title
Leisure Britain
Commissioned by
John Csaky, Richard Harris
Client
Fitch & Co

The artist was asked to design a leisure map of Great Britain. This illustration was the central decorative part of a large wall map which contained detailed information about leisure activities in Great Britain.

Ink. 39 × 58.5 cms.

Christopher Wormell

Title
Chicken Pie
Commissioned by
Mary Lewis
Design Group
Lewis Moberly
Client
Buxted Poultry

The artist was asked to create a decorative border and individual vignettes to work in sympathy with photography on a range of chicken pies.

Wood engraving. 12 × 7 cms.

SWAN & SALMON

Andrew Davidson

Title
Swan and Salmon
Commissioned by
David Stuart
Design Group
The Partners
Client
John Smith's Tadcaster
Brewery Ltd

The Partners were asked to create a visually cohesive and exciting range of pub signs which would give the brewery a striking corporate identity. Several illustrators were commissioned to depict the pub titles. They were asked to use silhouetted images and to inject a spark of humour into the illustrations by looking at the subject from a new angle.

Overlays used for printing onto enamel. 31 × 27 cms.

Carol Lawson

Title
Christmas Postbox
Commissioned by
Peter Windett
Design Group
Peter Windett & Associates
Client
Crabtree & Evelyn

The artist was asked to produce
an illustration from a visual
supplied by the design group
representing a Victorian postbox.
The illustration had to work 'in
the round' and the client wanted
an authentic Victorian
atmosphere about the children
and their costumes.

Watercolour, gouache.
26 × 40 cms.

Grahame Baker

Title
Shopfront
Commissioned by
Malcolm Hatton
Design Group
Splash of Paint
Client
Michael Bracken Fabrics

An illustration was required for an A6 card to promote this shop which sells high quality textiles. The illustrator was asked to produce a colourful, decorative and semi-abstract painting, resembling a fabric design, of the shopfront.

Inks, acrylic. 22.5 × 29 cms.

Jonathan Field

Title
Trafalgar Square
Commissioned by
Bill Wallsgrove
Design Group
Coley Porter Bell and Partners
Client
Fox's Biscuits Ltd

The artist was asked to produce
an alternative view of a famous
landmark. The illustration had to
include a reference to Fox's
biscuits and was used on a
biscuit tin lid.

Conté crayon, gouache.
60 × 50 cms.

Jeffrey Fisher

Title
Leading Edge
Commissioned by
Kate Stephens
Design Group
Wolff Olins
Client
3i

The artist was asked to illustrate the cover for a brochure conveying the impression that the investment company, 3i, is at the leading edge of business.

Watercolour, ink. 45 × 29 cms.

George Hardie

Title
The Works
Commissioned by
Ian Cockburn
Client
Trickett and Webb

The artist was asked for an interpretation of 'The Works', for the design group's calendar.

Silkscreen print. 19.5 × 26 cms.

Bush Hollyhead

Title
A New Beginning—Making the
Right Connection
Commissioned by
Stuart Baron
Design Group
David Davies Associates
Client
Midland Bank PLC

The artist was asked to provide
an illustration for the section
'Making the Right Connection'
in the Midland Bank retirement
brochure. This section suggests
books and leaflets to read and
organisations to join, which help
people embarking on
retirement—a new stage in life.

Watercolour, crayon.
45 × 35 cms.

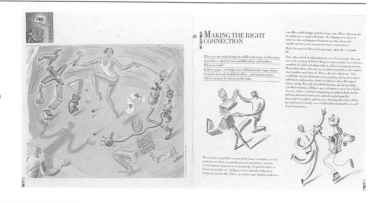

Chris Madden

Title
The Balance of Terror
Commissioned by
Corrine Gray
Client
Spark Communications

The poster called for an
illustration to convey the
aggressive, confrontational
posturing of the super powers
and the perilous instability of the
continual build-up of nuclear
arms.

Dip pen and ink. 42 × 29.5 cms.

Siobhan Keaney

Title
Sharp Practice
Commissioned by
Mary Lewis
Design Group
Lewis Moberly
Client
Sharp Practice

The artist was asked to create a logo for the new illustrators' agency, Sharp Practice.

Pen and ink. 11.5 × 11.5 cms.

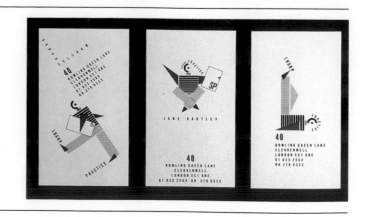

INFORMATION AND TECHNICAL

Information and Technical Judging Panel
Peter Cull FMAA, Hon FIMBI, SBStJ,
Director of Audio Visual Teaching Unit,
Robin Brook Centre, St Bartholomew's
Hospital; Stuart Jackman, Art Director,
Dorling Kindersley Ltd; Tom Liddell,
Deputy Head of the Division of Technical
and Scientific Illustration at Blackpool and
Fylde College; Ian Penney, illustrator; Lisa
Tai, Art Editor, Octopus Books.

David Penney

Title
Omega Olympic Chronograph
Watch
Commissioned by
Martin Suter
Agency
Stalder & Suter
Client
Omega

The artist had to show the
function and 'feeling' of this
modern skeletonised version of
the original 1936 Olympic
Games timekeeper. A limited
edition print was sent to selected
Omega clients.

Airbrushed watercolour.
30 × 30 cms.

AWARD

DRG
**ROYAL SOVEREIGN
GRAPHICS**

DEVILBISS ®

This artist has been selected to
receive the Royal Sovereign/
DeVilbiss Award for Excellence
in the Use of Airbrush.

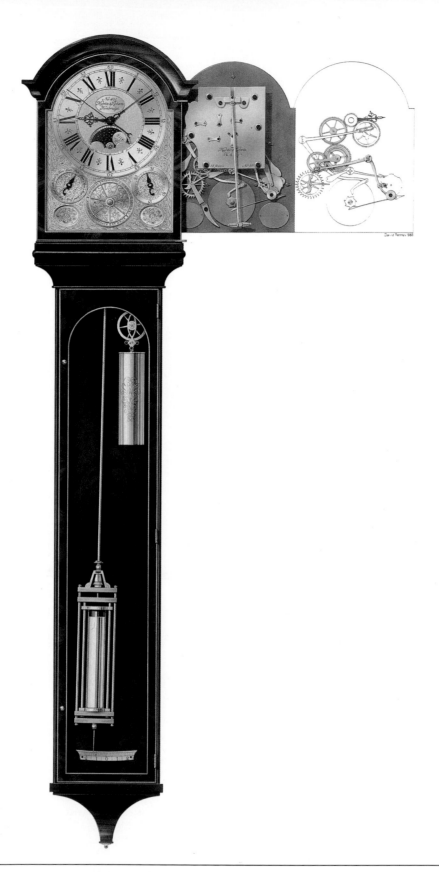

David Penney

Title
Martin & Roberts Wall
Regulator

This was a private commission
from the owner of this unique
clock. The artist shows the
function and 'feeling' of this
modern precision wall clock with
a perpetual calendar mechanism.

Airbrushed watercolour.
75 × 50 cms.

Cheryl Wilbraham

Title
The Heathland

This illustration was produced in response to a scientific illustration brief at Blackpool and Fylde College. The student was asked to prepare an illustration of the heathland showing a comprehensive range of the flora and fauna natural to this habitat. The illustration would be used for a television documentary and would appear in a brochure accompanying the programme.

Watercolour. 59.5 × 84 cms.

Steven Holden

Title
The Hedgerow

This illustration was produced in response to a scientific illustration brief at Blackpool and Fylde College. The student was asked to prepare an illustration of the contents of the hedgerow suitable for publication in 'The Young Naturalist'; a section of a Sunday supplement which encourages young people to become aware of their natural environment. Soil samples were analysed and drawings prepared from laboratory studies.

Watercolour, gouache.
42 × 59.5 cms.

David Hall

Title
The Hedgerow

This illustration was produced in response to a scientific illustration brief at Blackpool and Fylde College. The student was asked to prepare an illustration of the contents of the hedgerow, suitable for publication in 'The Young Naturalist'; a section of a Sunday supplement which encourages young people to become aware of their natural environment. Soil samples were analysed and drawings prepared from laboratory studies.

Watercolour. 59.5 × 84 cms.

FILM

Director
Matt Forrest
Animators
Big Features
Title
Stephen Duffy 'Kiss Me'
Production Company
Snapper Films @ MGM
Commissioned by
Donna Thomson
Client
Ten Records

A live action and animated film interpreting 'A 4 Minute Kiss'.

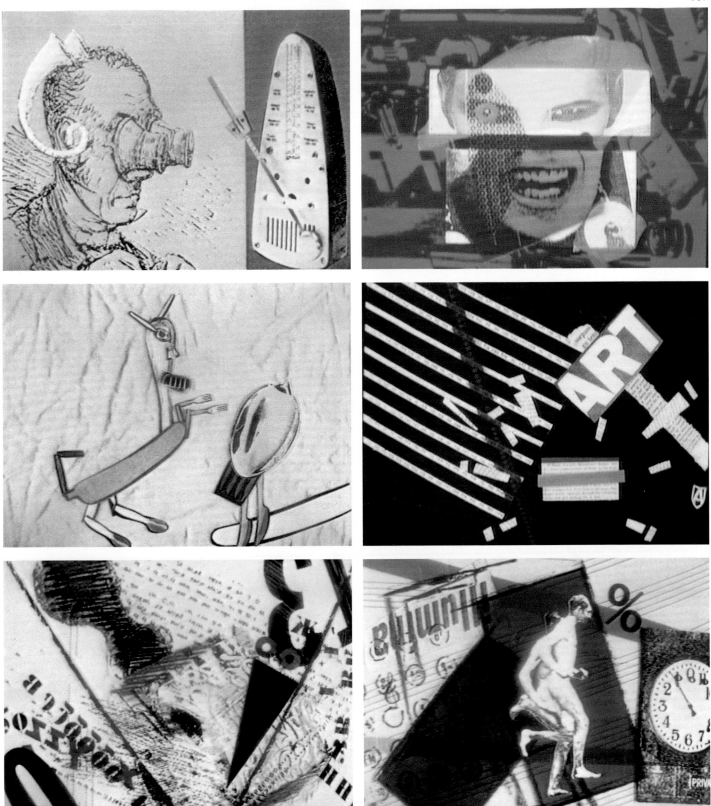

Director
Matt Forrest
Animators
Big Features
Title
Art of Noise 'Close to the Edit'
Production Company
Snapper Films @ MGM
Commissioned by
Paul Morley
Client
Island Records/ZTT

A pop promo for the Art of Noise.

Director/Animator
Karen Kelly
Title
Aikido

The 2 minute film was the culmination of a college project on Aikido. Its aim was to be an introduction to the graceful and flowing nature of the Japanese martial art which the illustrator felt was best expressed through the use of animation. The artist is a student at Harrow College of Higher Education.

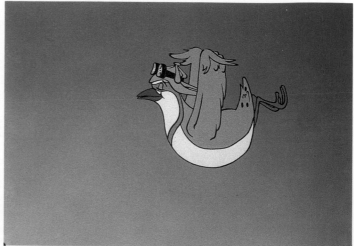

Directors
John Miller, Paul Vester
Animators
Bobbie Clennell, John Miller
Title
Heineken 'Partridge'
Production Company
Speedy Cartoons Ltd
Design
Chuck Jones
Backgrounds
Sue Branch

Camera
Cartoon Camera Company
Editing
Picturehead Productions
Commissioned by
Kevin Jones, Paul Hodgkinson,
Mike Griffin
Agency
Lowe Howard Spink Marschalk
Client
Whitbread & Co. PLC

A 40 second T.V. commercial in the style of a Warner Brothers cartoon. The film has a soundtrack based on 'The Twelve Days of Christmas', sung in a voice reminiscent of Bing Crosby.

UNPUBLISHED

Unpublished Judging Panel

Professional

Mel Calman, cartoonist; Sarah Culshaw,
artists' agent, Sharp Practice; Paul Garrett,
Art Director, Braybrooks & Garrett; Bob
Norrington, illustrator and designer; Jean-
Paul Tibbles, illustrator.

Student

Tony Clayden, Head of the Department of
Graphic Design, Exeter College of Art &
Design; Jacqui Figgis, artists' agent; Peter
Green, Art Director, VNU Business
Publications; Fiona MacVicar, illustrator and
tutor; Paul Wright, illustrator and tutor.

Debbie Lush

Title
1930's Buildings

This is one in a series of illustrations exploring the shapes of 1930's architecture. The intention was to portray the atmosphere they evoke today. The artist is a student at Harrow School of Art.

Tissue paper, pen, bleach.
44 × 30 cms.

AWARD

This illustration has been selected to receive the 1986 Beresford Sherman Award for the Best Unpublished Illustration.

Siân Edwards

Title
Dog

'Dog' is one of a series of drawings illustrating elements of aggression, drama and fear present physically and psychologically in daily urban life. The artist is a student at the Royal College of Art.

Pastel and graphite.
58 × 76 cms.

AWARD

FITCH
&COMPANY
DESIGN
CONSULTANTS PLC

This artist has been selected to receive the 1986 Fitch Award for the Most Promising Newcomer.

Julie Douglas

Title
May

The college brief asked the
students to produce a set of
drawings for a calendar. The
artist chose to produce an image
of herself for each month without
naming that month. The artist is
a student at Norwich School of
Art.

Coloured pencil.
15.5 × 20.5 cms.

AWARD

**REXEL
CUMBERLAND**

This illustration has been
selected to receive The 1986
Rexel Cumberland Award for the
Best Coloured Pencil
Illustration.

Julie Douglas

Title
The Little Drummer Girl

This is one of a set of
illustrations entered for the 1985
Young Illustrators Competition
sponsored by Reader's Digest
Condensed Books and organised
by the AOI. The brief was to
illustrate four pages of the novel
with freshness and originality.
The artist is a student at
Norwich School of Art.

Coloured pencil. 25.5 × 38 cms.

Stephen Wilkin

Title
The Bee on the Comb

The illustration is a visual answer to the challenge set by Kit Williams to find the title of his recent book. The artist is a student at Manchester Polytechnic.

Gouache. 25 × 19.5 cms.

Gary Keane

Title
Laurence Hunter

The painting was commissioned
by Laurence Hunter to hang in
his boardroom.

Acrylic. 100 × 68 cms.

Jon Liddell

Title
The Shed

The scientific illustration brief for this piece was to illustrate the importance of old buildings in providing shelter for a wealth of animal and insect life during the hibernation. The illustration would be used in a brochure and as a poster for the Nature Conservancy Council to encourage preservation of these sites and the related wildlife. The artist is a student at Blackpool and Fylde College.

46.5 × 58 cms.

Colin Rispin

Title
Fast Food—Please!

This illustration was designed to contrast the plight of the Third World against the opulence of the throw-away, fast-food society of the West.

Acrylic. 28 × 20.5 cms.

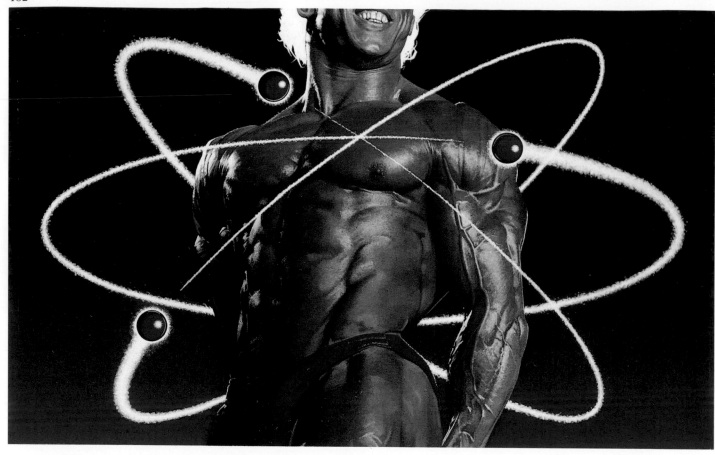

George Marshall

Title
Energy

The illustration was entered for
the 1985 Benson & Hedges
Illustrators Gold Awards.
Competitors were asked to
interpret the theme Energy. The
artist is a student at Manchester
Polytechnic.

Acrylic. 32 × 20.5 cms.

George Marshall

Title
Still Life

This is a self promotional piece.
The artist's intention was to
produce a traditional still life.
The artist is a student at
Manchester Polytechnic.

Acrylic. 21 × 21.5 cms.

Leon Evans

Title
Fresh Food

The brief for this college project
was to produce an illustration for
the British Food Advisory Board
to promote fresh produce grown
in the British Isles. The
illustration would be published
as a half page advertisement in
'Healthy Living'. The artist is a
student at the North East Wales
Institute, Wrexham.

Oil on canvas board.
37 × 27 cms.

Leon Evans

Title
Cabbage and Fruit

The brief for this college project was to produce an illustration for the British Food Advisory Board to promote fresh produce grown in the British Isles. The illustration would be published as a single page advertisement in 'Healthy Living'. The artist is a student at the North East Wales Institute, Wrexham.

Oil on canvas board.
33.5 × 25.5 cms.

Allan Manham

Title
Still Life

A self promotional piece.

Oil. 38 × 50 cms.

Joanna Cameron

Title
Brent Geese in Chichester
Harbour

The brief for this natural history illustration was to portray Brent geese in one of their Winter habitats after having migrated South. The artist had to give an accurate description of their plumage, stance, movement and marshland habitat. The artist is a student at St. Bartholomew's Medical Hospital.

Watercolour. 44.5 × 69 cms.

Simon Thompson

Title
Farmhouse Kitchen

The artist set himself a brief to
illustrate an article in a magazine
about farmhouse cooking. The
artist wanted to convey the
different textures of the objects
by the use colour and line. The
work was done while the artist
was a student at the North East
Wales Institute, Wrexham.

Coloured pencil. 30 × 46 cms.

Simon Thompson

Title
Fresh Cream Cakes

This illustration was produced while the artist was still a student at the North East Wales Institute, Wrexham. He was set a still life composition of cream cakes to draw which had to be made to look fresh and appealing.

Coloured pencil. 29.5 × 42 cms.

Mark O'Neill

Title
Dawn Chores

The illustration is one in a series
of self-promotional pieces based
upon the chores carried out by
the son of an Irish farmer.

Pastel, coloured pencil.
65 × 55 cms.

Mark O'Neill

Title
Snow Shoot

The illustration is one in a series
of self-promotional pieces based
upon the chores carried out by
the son of an Irish farmer.

Pastel, coloured pencil.
72 × 47 cm.

Simon Critchley

Title
Take a Train from the Ghetto

This was a self-imposed brief following an existing magazine grid structure. The artist wanted to convey how some of the great jazz musicians developed out of an environment of poverty and squalor. The illustration shows John Coltrane against a background of urban decay.

Gesso, gouache, pencil crayon.
51 × 34 cms.

Christopher White

Title
Spice Warehouses off Garnet
Street

This is one of a series of
drawings in a personal project
depicting the Thames
Embankment from Westminster
Bridge to the Thames Barrier.

Watercolour, pen. 85 × 60 cms.

Matthew Cook

Title
Kew Gardens

These location drawings of Kew Gardens were done as studies for a project to produce a promotional poster for London Underground. The artist is a student at Kingston Polytechnic.

Ink, wax crayon. 58.5 × 42 cms.

Brian Sanders

Title
5 Albermarle Villas

This painting was produced as a
Christmas present for a friend,
the owner of the house.

Watercolour. 61 × 38 cms.

Robert Altham

Title
The Snow Goose

This is one of a set of
illustrations awarded Highly
Commended in the 1985 Young
Illustrators' Competition
sponsored by Reader's Digest
and organised by the AOI. The
artist wanted to depict the
turbulence and insecurity
prevalent at the onset of the
Second World War and the
emotional bond between the
young girl and the snow goose.
The artist is a student at
Lancashire Polytechnic.

Oil. 48 × 33 cms.

Colin Stimpson

Title
The Snow Goose

This is one of a set of illustrations awarded Highly Commended in the 1985 Young Illustrators' Competition sponsored by Reader's Digest and organised by the AOI. The novel chosen, 'The Snow Goose' by Paul Gallico, had to be illustrated with freshness and originality.

Watercolour, crayon.
27 × 19 cms.

Annabel Wright

Title
Tenant's Kitchen

The illustration was produced in response to a college project to illustrate the conflict between landlord and tenant. This represents the tenant's point of view. The artist is a student at Brighton Polytechnic.

Mixed media collage.
41 × 52.5 cms.

Annabel Wright

Title
Landlady Descending a Staircase

The illustration was produced in response to a college project to illustrate the conflict between landlord and tenant. This represents the tenant's point of view. The artist is a student at Brighton Polytechnic.

Mixed media collage.
41 × 52.5 cms.

Martin Orme

Title
" 'Tes Flyin' in the Face of Nature"

This is one of a set of illustrations for the novel 'Cold Comfort Farm' by Stella Gibbons. The grotesque and comic characters here discuss how to "forstall the disastrous effect of too much sukebind and too many long summer evenings on the female system". The artist is a student at Leeds Polytechnic.

Watercolour, acrylic.
63 × 45.5 cms.

David Mitcheson

Title
Mr & Mrs R. Andrews &
Mrs Mopp

This illustration was produced to
accompany an imaginary article
which questions the authenticity
of certain old masters in art
galleries throughout the world.
The artist is a student at
Leicester Polytechnic.

Watercolour. 26 × 33 cms.

Dave McKean

Title
Francis Ford Coppola

This is one of a series of portraits of film directors completed for the artist's portfolio. The portraits relate to photography and are fundamentally monochrome. The artist says of this piece, "Coppola is a big man, in a big job with a big beard, who makes big films from equally big ideas. In places I wasn't sure where he finished and the background began." The artist is a student at Berkshire College of Art and Design.

Gouache, pencil, pastel, tissue paper. 50.5 × 70 cms.

Dulce Tobin

Title
Hiroshima Remembered

The illustration was produced in reaction to the 1985 media coverage of the bombing of Hiroshima and Nagasaki forty years previously. The artist wanted to represent the scarification of women's faces and of the country in one image. The artist is a student at Brighton Polytechnic.

Oil monoprint. 40.5 × 31.5 cms.

Carolyn Piggford

Title
All Quiet on the Western Front

During the Summer vacation the artist was asked to produce a series of illustrations based on trompe l'oeil. This book cover contains items referring to a soldier's life in combat. The artist is a student at Leeds Polytechnic.

Watercolour, gouache.
47.5 × 33 cms.

Helen Jones

Title
The Fall

In this book cover design for 'The Fall' by Albert Camus the artist was trying to capture the misty, moody atmosphere of Amsterdam and the dreamy quality of the writing. "Holland is a dream Monsieur, a dream of gold and smoke, smokier by day and more gilded by night." The artist is a student at St. Martins School of Art.

Ink. 7.5 × 15 cms.

Lorna Hussey

Title
The Cat who would be King

This is a proposed illustration for the book cover of a children's fantasy story. For reference the artist used the work of Holbein and Hilliard, in particular Hilliard's miniatures. The artist is a student at Manchester Polytechnic.

Acrylic. 21 × 12.5 cms.

Lorna Hussey

Title
Animal Band

This is an illustration proposed for the cover for a collection of anthropomorphic children's stories. The artist has looked to the composition and decoration of Indian painting and carpet work when composing this illustration. The artist is a student at Manchester Polytechnic.

Acrylic. 8 × 31 cms.

Gary Michael Bines

Title
Slaveships over Cantenaar

The artist was asked to illustrate a passage from his own story 'Tei Lum'. The passage chosen, which describes the great procession of Ketetsi slaveships preparing for the descent to Cantenaar, demanded an almost funereal air. The artist is a student at Cornwall Technical College.

Gouache. 43.5 × 31.5 cms.

Lawrence Zeegan

Title
Sikorsky

This illustration was produced in response to the news coverage in 1986 of the bid by Sikorsky for Westland Helicopters. The artist intended the illustration to be a deliberate contrast to serious journalism. The artist is a student at Camberwell School of Art and Crafts.

Silkscreen print. 63 × 45 cms.

David Lodge

Title
The Flame Trees of Thika I

This is one of a set of four illustrations awarded Third Prize in the 1985 Young Illustrators' Competition sponsored by Reader's Digest and organised by the AOI. The panel of judges were looking for illustrations showing freshness and originality. The artist is a student at Trent Polytechnic.

Photocopy, watercolour.
27 × 19 cms.

David Lodge

Title
The Flame Trees of Thika II

This is one of a set of four illustrations awarded Third Prize in the 1985 Young Illustrators' Competition sponsored by Reader's Digest and organised by the AOI. The panel of judges were looking for illustrations showing freshness and originality. The artist is a student at Trent Polytechnic.

Photocopy, watercolour.
27 × 19 cms.

Within the illustration:

WILSON HARRIS
CARNIVAL

The book typographer has the job of erecting a window between the reader inside the room and that landscape which is the author's words. He may put up a stained-glass window of marvellous beauty, but a failure as a window; that is, he may use some rich superb type like text gothic that is something to be looked at, not *through*. Or he may work in what I call transparent or invisible typography. I have a book at home, of which I have no visual recollection whatever as far as its typography goes; when I think of it, all I see is the Three Musketeers and their comrades swaggering up and down the streets of Paris. The third type of window is one in which the glass is broken into relatively small leaded panes; and this corresponds to what is called 'fine printing' today, in that you are at least conscious that there is a window there, and that someone has enjoyed building it. That is not objectionable, because of a very important fact which has to do with the psychology of the subconscious mind. This is that the mental eye focuses *through* type and not *upon* it. The type which, through any arbitrary warping of design or excess of 'colour', gets in the way of the mental picture to be conveyed, is a bad type. Our subconsciousness is always afraid of blunders (which illogical setting, tight spacing and too-wide unleaded lines can trick us into), of boredom, and of officiousness. The running headline that keeps shouting at us, the line that looks like one long word, the capitals jammed together without hair-spaces – these

ff
faber and faber

WILSON HARRIS *CARNIVAL*
ff

John Scott

Title
More Pricks than Kicks at
C.C.A.

The brief for this college project was flexible allowing the designer to interpret the theme as he thought fit. The novel illustration involves murder, mystery and sexual exploits. The artist is a student at Canterbury College of Art.

Mixed media. 28.5 × 21.5 cms.

Jason Godfrey

Title
The Sleeping Congregation

The illustrator's intention was to produce a contemporary interpretation of William Hogarth's engraving, 'The Sleeping Congregation'. The artist is a student at Brighton Polytechnic.

Lino, marker pen. 62 × 43 cms.

Matilda Harrison

Title
Dante's 'Inferno'

This illustration was produced in response to a college project to illustrate 'Hell on Earth'. The artist used a literary source to interpret this theme. The sinners are positioned in accordance with Dante's hierarchy in the 'Inferno'. The artist is a student at St. Martins School of Art.

Lino ink on acetate.
55 × 38 cms.

Matilda Harrison

Title
The Maids

This illustration is the result of a self-set project to illustrate 'The Maids' by Jean Genet. The artist was concerned with representing the ambiguity of roles in a 'film-noir' setting. The artist is a student at St. Martins School of Art.

Lino ink on acetate.
74 × 62.5 cms.

Brian Cairns

Title
Of Mice and Men

The artist set himself the project of illustrating the cover of John Steinbeck's novel. Elements from various chapters are combined to convey the atmosphere of the book. Colour is important in suggesting events and contributing to the overall 'feel'. The artist is a student at Glasgow School of Art.

Oil on canvas. 152.5 × 107 cms.

Gordon Hendry

Title
Portrait of a Painting Tutor

The college brief called for a portrait of an art school lecturer. The artist tried to concentrate on the distinction between a painter and a painting tutor and came up with a positive and lively solution. The artist is a student at Duncan and Jordanstone College of Art.

44 × 36 cms.

Tracey Chapman

Title
Fantasy on the Tube

The idea for this painting came from the artist studying men on the tube and imagining what they were thinking about. The man is carrying out his fantasy; he has his perfect woman, fame, and an endless supply of alcohol! The tube provides a novel place to locate this fantasy. The artist is a student at St. Martins School of Art.

Watercolour, pastel.
40 × 49 cms.

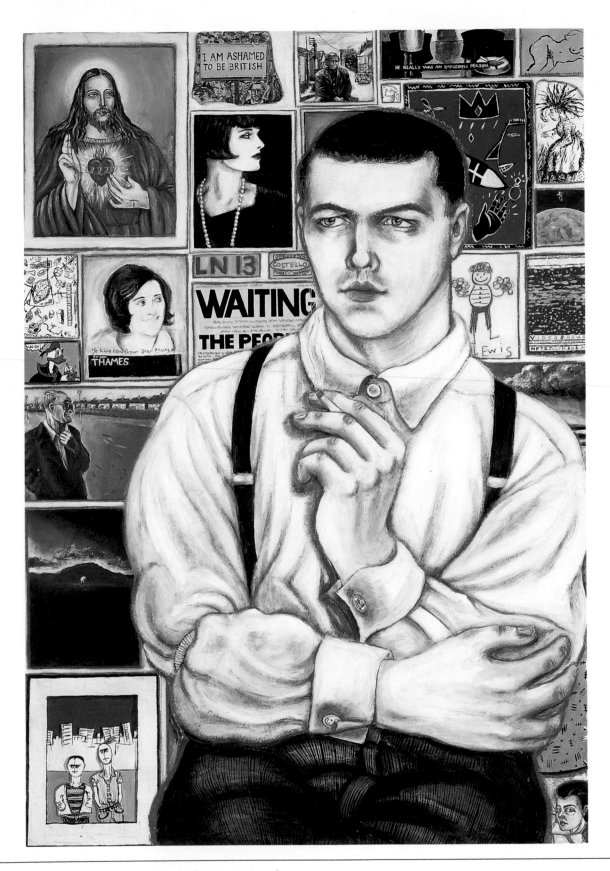

Matilda Harrison

Title
Lewis

This is the first in a series of portraits that incorporate important elements of the sitter's personality and history. The artist is a student at St. Martins School of Art.

Acrylic, pastel. 89.5 × 61.5 cms.

Peter Tucker

Title
Vin et Vigne

The illustration was produced in response to a college project to describe the process of wine making, from the grape in the vineyard to the bottle on the table. The artist is a student at Swindon College of Art and Design.

Gouache, coloured pencil.
35 × 232 cms.

Lynda Gray

Title
Liqueur Label

The artist was commissioned by
Frances Lovell at the Michael
Peters Group to produce a
bright, naïve Caribbean scene for
a wrap around label on a bottle of
Jamaican-style liqueur. The label
was not used.

Gouache. 14 × 48 cms.

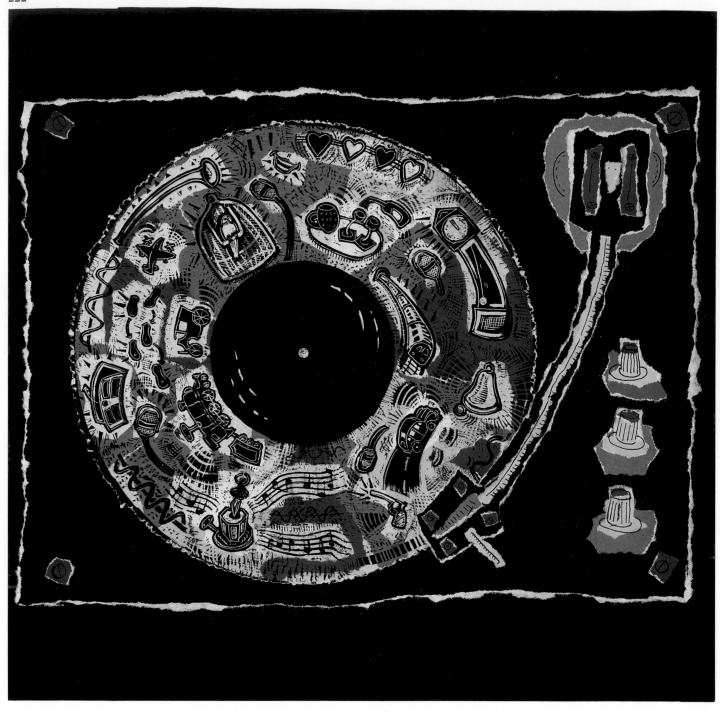

Michael Armson

Title
Sound Effects

This illustration was produced in response to a D & AD workshop project to illustrate a cover for a BBC sound effects record. The artist's intention was to show that sounds from disparate sources are brought together on one record. The artist is a student at Liverpool Polytechnic.

Scraperboard, collage.
30 × 24 cms.

Liverpool Polytechnic
Illustration
Degree Show 1986
Open Tuesday to Thursday, 24-26 June

Faculty of Art & Design, Myrtle Street, Liverpool L7 7DN

051-207 3581 ext 2901

Michael Armson

Title
Launch

This illustration was used to promote the 1986 degree show at Liverpool Polytechnic. The artist's intention was to illustrate the idea that a degree show is a starting point for its students. The artist is a student at Liverpool Polytechnic.

Scraperboard, screenprint.
59.5 × 42 cms.

Mary Roberts

Title
A Cocktail or Two

The artist set herself the project of providing an illustration to promote cocktails for a bar in Barbados.

Watercolour. 29 × 23 cms.

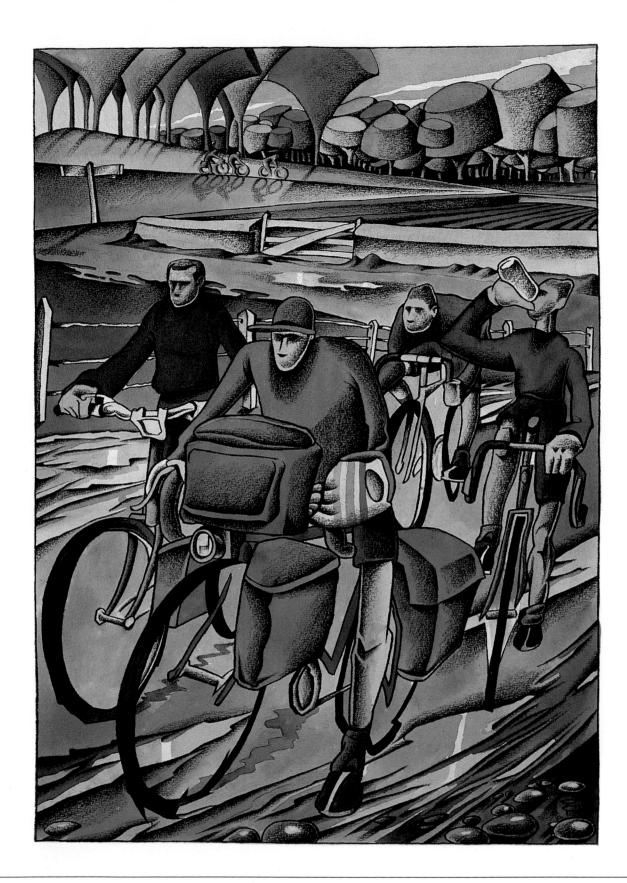

Fiona MacVicar

Title
Autumn Cyclists

The illustrator is a keen cyclist
and this self promotional piece is
one of several on a cycling theme.

Watercolour, conté pencil.
39.5 × 28 cms.

Tony Watson

Title
The Apostle Spoon

This drawing was produced after the artist had been told he should do more food drawings. Rather than draw a straightforward still life, the artist chose to incorporate a visual pun using the apostle spoon.

Pen and ink, watercolour.
20 × 14.5 cms.

place Jemaa El Fna. Marrakesh

Ian Pollock

Title
Man Pushing Woman on Cart

This is one of a series of
drawings inspired by visits to
North Africa.

Ink, plaka. 63 × 54 cms.

Max Ellis

Title
Frustration

This illustration is the result of a
personal project to produce a
graphic portrayal of mental
frustration. The artist uses
imagery of stress reinforced by
harsh line to convey frustration.
The artist is a student at
Brighton Polytechnic.

Acrylic and ballpoint pen.
29 × 22 cms.

Paul Dickinson

Title
Black Silk

This illustration was
commissioned by Michael
Woodward Associates for a
poster. It has not yet been
published.

Pencil, ink. 45 × 29 cms.

André Yaniw

Title
Saturday Night, Sunday Morning

The illustration is for Alan Sillitoe's study of post-war morality, 'Saturday Night, Sunday Morning'. It is a self promotional piece for the artist's portfolio.

Gouache, coloured pencil.
31 × 26 cms.

Liz Roberts

Title
Girl Drawing

This was a personal project to
draw friends at work in their own
environment. The illustration
was used on the poster launching
The Guitty Talberg Agency.

Watercolour, ink. 30 × 21 cms.

Andrew Stewart Brown

Title
Sitting in the Sun

The illustration depicts the
typical late middle-aged couple
found at British sea-side holiday
resorts.

Coloured pencil. 24 × 29.5 cms.

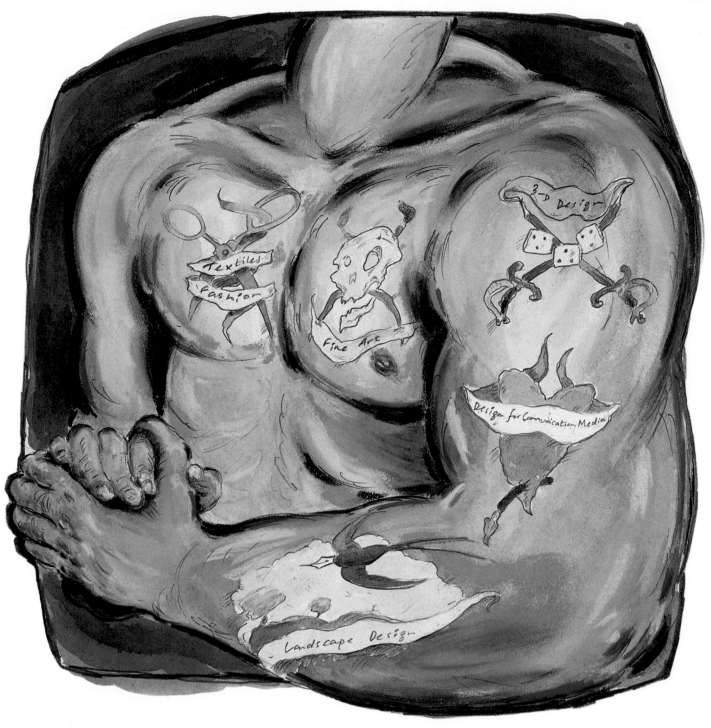

Michael O'Shaughnessy

Title
A Degree of Muscle

This illustration was produced to promote the Art and Design degree show. The artist is a student at Manchester Polytechnic.

Watercolour, chalk pastel. 28 × 28 cms.

John Hargreaves

Title
Abdul's Take-away and Paradise
Restaurant

This is one of a series of
drawings intending to show the
way in which some of
Manchester's drab Victorian
buildings have been exotically
transformed since their
occupation by Asian traders.
Coloured pencils were used for
their liveliness of mark making to
produce a bold and cheerful
drawing. The artist is a student at
Manchester Polytechnic.

Coloured pencil. 39 × 39 cms.

Jonathan Field

Title
The First Glimpse of the Sea

This is one of a series of
illustrations for a short story,
produced with a view to
publication in the future.

Gouache, conté crayon, pastel.
48 × 38 cms.

Mark Oldroyd

Title
Love and Death No.5—Marilyn
Monroe

This is one illustration for a
project, 'Aspects of Love and
Death'. The artist wished to
study how societies react to the
death of well-known
personalities whether they be
politicians or film stars. The
artist is a student at St. Martins
School of Art.

Acrylic. 56 × 55 cms.

Index

The Association of Fashion, Advertising and Editorial Photographers represents the majority of advertising and magazine photographers in the United Kingdom. The Association was formed to protect the rights and promote the interests of its members, to encourage a high standard of professionalism and ethical behaviour, and to promote the interest in and use of photography by both the industry and the general public. We believe in the need for these Awards in order to create a precise look at the best of photography produced by members in one of the most prestigious photographers' associations in the world. We wish to eliminate our reliance upon the goodwill of other bodies to acknowledge our work, so that photography may be seen in its own terms rather than in relation to design or art direction.

All work shown here has been selected, out of over seven hundred entries, by seven judges representing the different fields to which the members of our Association contribute. Gold has been awarded to photographs the judges felt showed such a uniqueness of concept and originality as to make them potential classics, and viewed as such in years to come. Silvers were awarded to photographs that, though they showed originality and expertise, lacked the uniqueness for a Gold Award. Merits were awarded when the work showed an idea, approach or concept that necessitated a mention beyond that of being selected for the exhibition.

It will, we hope, increase the prestige of the medium, the Association and its individual members, while at the same time offering to the public a viewing which would otherwise go unseen.

We would like to thank the following, who have helped us with their time and effort, and the membership of the Association whose support makes the AFAEP Awards possible.

JUDGES
Ken Griffiths   Angus McBean
John Hegarty   Ray Massey
Mike Lackersteen   James Wedge
Paul Leeves

ORGANISERS
Bryce Attwell   Nicky Newman
Desmond Burdon   Alison Theaker
Janet Ibbotson   Adam Woolfitt

Also thanks to
Richard Apperley   Nick Knight
Ron Bagley   Colin Mills
Simon Bishop   Paul Robinson
Robert Golden   Peter Rose
Dave Kampfner   Pentagram

AFAEP AWARDS

CONTENTS

SPONSORSHIP

Advertising: Food/Drink – CETA LIMITED
Advertising: General Still Life – BENSON & HEDGES
Advertising: Interiors/Exteriors – FUJI PROFESSIONAL
Advertising: People– KEITH JOHNSON PHOTOGRAPHIC
Advertising: Landscape – GOOD HOUSEKEEPING'S
   COUNTRY LIVING
Editorial: People – OLYMPUS UK LIMITED
Personal: People – HASSELBLAD UK LIMITED
Personal: Places – NIKON UK LIMITED
Portfolio – KODAK LIMITED
Awards Night – ILFORD UK LIMITED

Left to right Ray Massey, Paul Leeves, Ken Griffiths, John Hegarty, Mike Lackersteen, James Wedge and Angus McBean

JUDGES

Angus McBean *Photographer*
McBean is known as the greatest theatrical photographer and Britain's best known surrealist. All of his photography – whether made in the theatre or in the studio – is totally romantic portrait photography.

He came to London in 1925, and worked as an antique restorer for seven years. His spare time was devoted to model making and photography. He received his first photographic commission in the theatre in 1936. His surrealist portraits of leading celebrities were immensely popular.

Through the 40s and 50s he was the official photographer at Stratford, The Royal Opera House, Sadlers Wells, Glyndebourne and the Old Vic.

In the 60s a variety of pop stars posed for sessions with McBean. At the age of seventy, he officially retired, and sold his London home and last studio to Harvard University.

Coaxed out of retirement in 1983 by the French Magazine, *L'Official*, he also completed a series of pictures for French *Vogue*. He continued undertaking commissions from the pop and fashion worlds into his eighties when – in lasting commemoration of his genius – his favourite studio portrait of Vivien Leigh was chosen to be reproduced as a postage stamp.

Mike Lackersteen *Art Director, Redwood Publishing*
Lackersteen was born in Singapore, came to Britain to start secondary education and then studied graphics at The London College of Printing. Upon leaving he worked at Corgi Books and Haymarket Publishing. Next came the jump to consumer magazines and *Good Housekeeping*, where he was assistant Art Editor for a short time before being made Art Director.

Four and a half years later he joined Redwood Publishing as Art Director, responsible for titles as diverse as *Expression*, *Airport*, *Intercity*, *Venture UK* and *Acorn User*.

In 1985 he was judged Magazine Designer of the Year by the British Society of Magazine Editors.

Ray Massey *Photographer*
Massey attended Somerset College of Art followed by three years at Medway College of Design. After a period of assisting, he started as a freelance photographer in 1970 working mainly as a reportage and editorial photographer.

He started a studio in Camden in 1971 and built a reputation for solving problems and consequently most of his work is not straight photography.

A large proportion of recent work has been for international clients in Europe and in the USA.

John Hegarty *Creative Director, Bartle Bogle Hegarty*
Hegarty joined Benton and Bowles as a junior Art Director in 1965, and left to join John Collings and Ptns for two and a half years. From there he joined the Cramer Saatchi consultancy and later became a founding shareholder in Saatchi and Saatchi. In 1979 he left to found TBWA as Creative Director, and worked on Ovaltine advertising, Lego, Johnny Walker Black Label and Schweppes, to name a few. His awards include two D&AD Golds and three Silvers, Campaign Gold award, three Clios, two Cannes Silver Lions and Creative Circle Commendations.

He left TBWA in 1982 to start BBH as Creative Director.

James Wedge *Photographer*
After attending the Royal College of Art, and without any specific photographic training, he started working as a freelance photographer in 1970.

He built a reputation for hand colouring which led him on to specialising in fashion, editorial and advertising, notably with work for *The Sunday Times*, *Cosmopolitan*, Russell & Bromley and Wrangler Jeans.

Paul Leeves *Creative Director, Boase Massimi Pollitt*
Leeves entered advertising in 1964 and became an art director in 1970 with Aalders Marchant Weinreich where he won his first awards. He moved on to Kirkwoods and then Greys in Sydney. On his return to the UK he became partner and Creative Director of Aalders Marchant.

He joined BMP as deputy Creative Director in 1983 and became joint Creative Director in 1984. Paul has won major awards in TV, Cinema, Press, Posters and design.

Ken Griffiths
Ken Griffiths was born in New Zealand. He studied at the Royal College of Art, and his first major assignment as a photographer was for the *Sunday Telegraph Magazine*.

He works mostly on location and always uses plate cameras. His distinctive style can be seen in numerous advertisements.

ADVERTISING

Andreas Heumann

Art Director
Mike Cavers
Client
Singer Sewing Machines
Agency
Cato Johnson

Stak Aivaliotis

Art Director
Ron Brown
Agency
Abbott Mead Vickers
Client
Kaye Shoes
Purpose
Press advertising

SILVER

CETA

Graham Ford

Title
Steak and kidney pie
Art Director
Nigel Rose
Agency
Collett Dickenson Pearce
Client
Atora
Purpose
Advertising
Background
Gordon Aldred
Media
Press

Peter Williams

Title
Mr. Punch
Agency
McCann Erickson
Client
William Grant and Sons Ltd
Purpose
Advertisement for Glenfiddich
Malt Whisky
Media
Punch Magazine

MERIT

BENSON and HEDGES

Graham Ford

Title
Cat and Goldfish Bowl
Art Director
Nigel Rose
Agency
Collett Dickenson Pearce
Client
Benson and Hedges
Purpose
Advertising
Media
Press & Poster

Paul Bussell

Title
Gold Screw
Art Director
Stan Codling
Agency
Dorland Advertising
Client
Poster sales
Media
48 Sheet Poster
Modelmakers
Metro Models
Background
Joe Lyons

Stak Aivaliotis ————————

Title
Bull and Bear
Art Director
Garry Horner
Agency
Collett Dickenson Pearce
Client
Apricot Computers
Purpose
Advertising
Media
Press

GOLD

Bob Miller ————

Art Director
Ron Brown
Agency
Abbott Mead Vickers/SMS Ltd
Client
Volvo
Writer
David Abbott
Purpose
Advertising
Media
Press

SILVER

Bob Miller

Art Director
Ron Brown
Agency
Abbott Mead Vickers/SMS Ltd
Client
Volvo
Writer
David Abbott
Purpose
Advertising
Media
Press

Bob Miller

Art Director
Russell Weiles
Agency
J. Walter Thompson
Client
Brooke Bond
Purpose
Press Ad

Bob Miller

Art Director
Ken Hoggins
Agency
Lowe Howard-Spink
Client
AC Delco
Writer
Chris O'Shea
Media
Poster

Bob Miller

Art Director
David George
Agency
Lowe Howard-Spink
Client
AC Delco
Media
Press

Robert Dowling

Art Director
Graham Westmoreland
Agency
Brahms
Client
ERF Trucks
Set
Terry Kemble

Alan Brooking

Title
Guayaquil, Ecuador
Art Director
Marco Calant
Agency
Publicis, Brussels
Client
Nestlé
Purpose
Press campaign for Nescafé

Spencer Rowell

Art Director
Mark Ready
Agency
Holmes Knight Ritchie
Client
Polygram
Media
Billboard

Sanders Nicolson

(pages 260—263)

Art Director
Steve Morris
Agency
Morris, Nicolson and Cartwright
Client
J. Barbour & Sons Ltd
Media
Press and Poster

SILVER

Tony Latham

Title
Dry Stone Walling
Art Director
Nigel Deegan
Agency
Paling Ellis KPR
Client
MSD
Purpose
Advertising

Graham Ford

Title
Girl and Porcupine
Art Director
Mike Shaffron
Agency
Saatchi and Saatchi
Client
Mail on Sunday
Purpose
Advertising
Media
Poster and Press

Stak Aivaliotis

Title
Rear View
Art Director
John Hegarty
Agency
Bartle Bogle Hegarty
Client
Dr. Whites
Media
Press

SILVER

Good Housekeeping's
COUNTRY LIVING

Duncan Sim

Art Director
Reg Pine
Agency
Ogilvy and Mather
Client
Ford

MERIT

COUNTRY LIVING

GOOD HOUSEKEEPING'S

Alan Brooking

Title
Wiltshire Dawn
Art Director
Neil Godfrey
Agency
Collett Dickenson Pearce
Client
Army Officer
Media
Press and Print

John Claridge

Title (below)
Route 1658
Art Director
John Claridge
Client
John Claridge Studio
Purpose
Direct mail poster

Title (top)
Moon
Art Director
Ken Scott
Agency
DDM Advertising
Client
Peugeot Ltd
Purpose
Brochure
Brief
Speed

MERIT

GOOD HOUSEKEEPING'S
COUNTRY LIVING

Alan Brooking

Title
Shark-O Straits, Hong Kong
Agency
Collett Dickenson Pearce
Client
Army Nursing Corps
Purpose
Speculative campaign
Media
Press

Duncan Sim

Art Director
Jeremy Haines
Agency
Smith and Milton
Client
Nat West

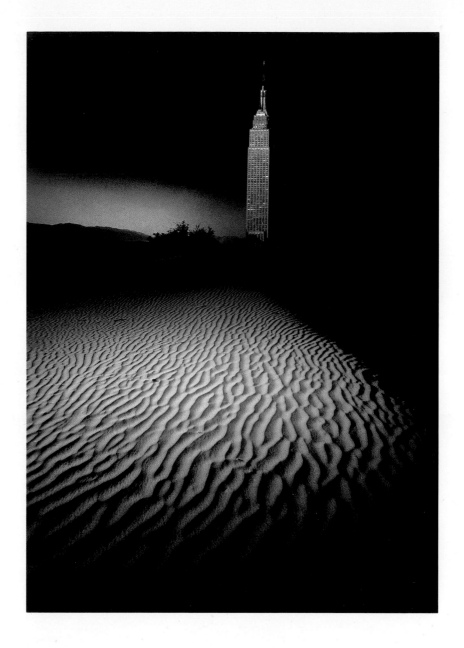

John Claridge

Title
New York
Art Director
John Claridge
Client
John Claridge Studio
Purpose
Direct Mail Poster

John Claridge

Title
Leopard
Art Director
John Claridge
Client
John Claridge Studio
Purpose
Direct Mail Poster

Title (top)
Empire State
Art Director
John Claridge
Client
John Claridge Studio
Purpose
Direct Mail Poster

John Claridge

Title
Bridge
Art Director
Ken Scott
Agency
DDM Advertising Ltd
Client
Peugeot Ltd
Purpose
Brochure
Brief
Engineering

EDITORIAL

Chris Simpson

Title
Luminescent
Client
Observer Colour Magazine
Purpose
Editorial

Chris Simpson

Title
Luminescent
Client
Observer Colour Magazine
Purpose
Editorial

Barry Lategan

Title
Lei Magazine 1984

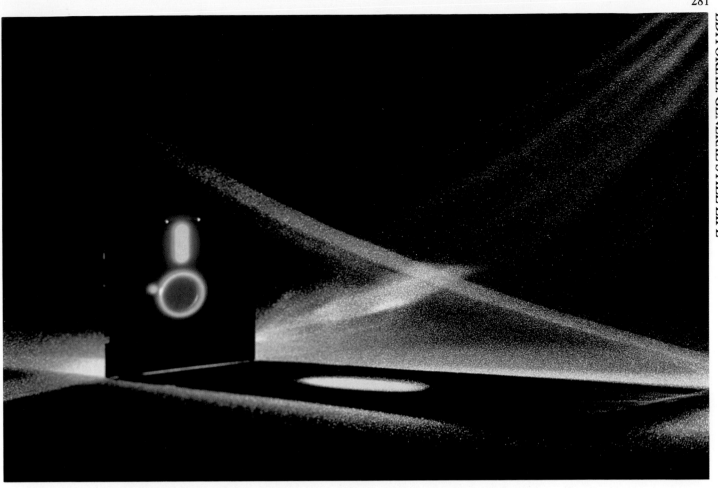

George Logan

Title
Floppy Disc
Art Director
Steve Palmer at Chintz Design
Client
Which Computer?
Media
Magazine
Brief
Open brief to illustrate article on
software

MERIT

John Brown

Client
A la Carte magazine, IPC
Purpose
Editorial
Media
Magazine

MERIT

John Brown

Client
A la Carte magazine, IPC
Purpose
Editorial
Media
Magazine

SILVER

OLYMPUS CAMERAS

Cornel Lucas

Title
Film Director and Producer,
Michael Powell & Emeric
Pressburger
Client
British Film Year
Purpose
Editorial and Exhibition

Cornel Lucas

Title
Film Director—David Lean
Client
British Film Year
Purpose
Editorial and Exhibition

MERIT

Trevor Wood

Client
Camera Magazine (EMAP)

John Claridge

Title
Ireland: A week in the life of a
nation
Art Director
Red Saunders and Syd Shelton
Client
Century Hutchinson Publishers
Purpose
Book

John Claridge

Title
Ireland: A week in the life of a
nation
Art Director
Red Saunders and Syd Shelton
Client
Century Hutchinson Publishers
Purpose
Book

John Claridge

Title
Ireland: A week in the life of a
nation
Art Director
Red Saunders and Syd Shelton
Client
Century Hutchinson Publishers
Purpose
Book

PERSONAL
NON-COMMISSIONED

SILVER

Tim Simmons

Purpose
Personal Work

MERIT

George Wright

Title
Tolpuddle Martyrs
Purpose
From a personal exhibition
Two Views From Dorset

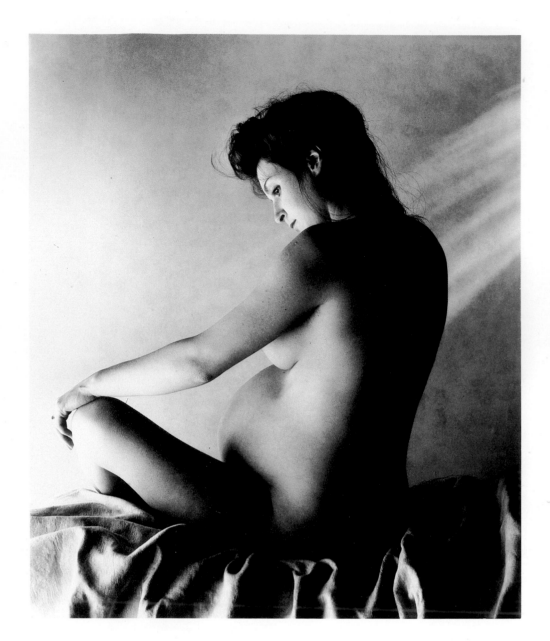

MERIT

Peter Myers

Purpose
Personal non-commissioned

John Claridge

Title
Firebird
Purpose
Personal

GOLD

Ron Bambridge

Purpose
Personal, self-promotional
Lake District and North Wales

GOLD

Ron Bambridge

Purpose
Personal, self-promotional
Lake District and North Wales

Ron Bambridge

Purpose
Personal, self-promotional
Lake District and North Wales

GOLD

Nikon

Ron Bambridge

Purpose
Personal, self-promotional
Lake District and North Wales

SILVER

Jonathan Trapman

Title
Icerink, NYC
Purpose
Personal

MERIT

Duncan Sim ——————— *Purpose*
Personal

MERIT

Chris Ryan

Title
Dal Lake, Kashmir
Purpose
Personal
Printer
Rod Bayles at Quicksilver

Chris Cheetham

Title
Sicily
Client
Chris Cheetham
Purpose
Self-promotion

Duncan Sim

(pages 304, 5, 6)

Purpose
Personal

Duncan Sim

Purpose
Personal

Trevor Wood

Purpose
Personal
Location
King's Lynn, setting for Hugh
Hudson's film 'Revolution'

Frank Herholdt

Title
Bhubaneswar Market
Purpose
Personal Work, my holiday snaps

Andreas Heumann

Title
Sylt 1984
Printer
Andreas Heumann

John Claridge

Title
Trees
Purpose
Personal work

John Claridge

Title (above)
Yellow Truck
Purpose
Personal work

Title (opposite page)
Docks
Purpose
Personal work

John Claridge

Title
New York Bar
Purpose
Personal

MERIT

David Stewart ———— *Purpose*
Personal, non-commissioned

MERIT

John Turner ———————— *Purpose*
Personal work

MERIT

Chris Cheetham

Title
Coffee Pot
Client
Chris Cheetham
Purpose
Self-promotion

MERIT

John Shaw

Title
Chair in Leaf
Client
Self
Purpose
Self-promotion

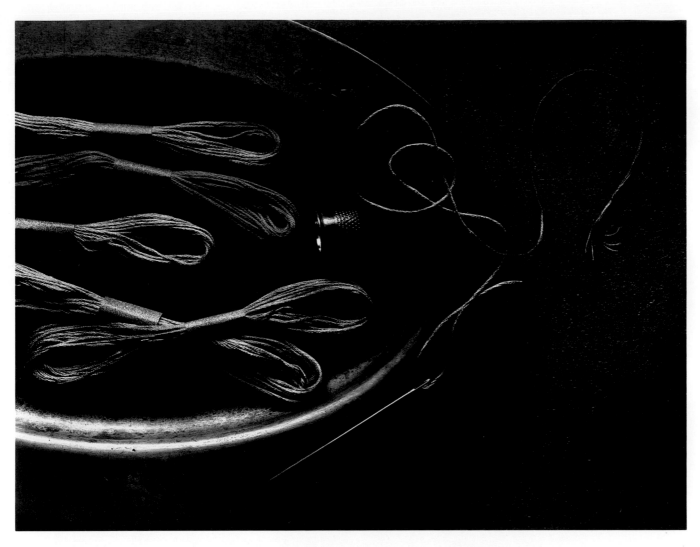

Mike Botha

Purpose
Personal non-commissioned

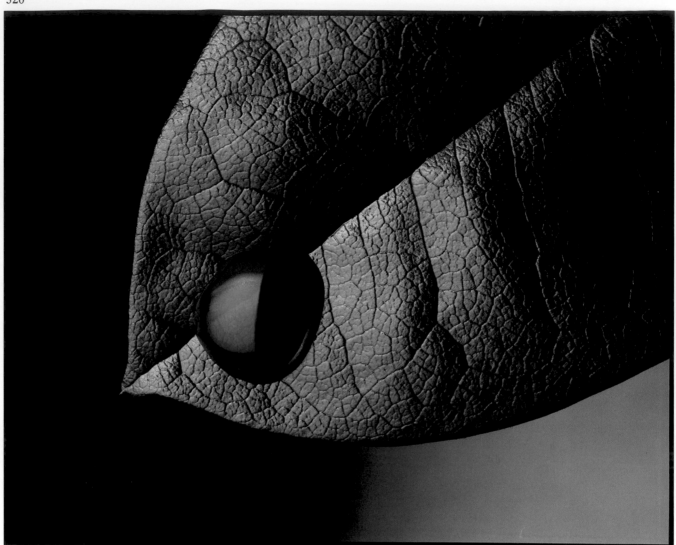

Julian Nieman

Title
Leaf and Rainbow Drop
Purpose
Self-brief personal work

Julian Nieman

Title
Brush and Rainbow Drop
Purpose
Self-brief personal work

Jess Koppel

Purpose
Personal non-commissioned
photograph

David Stewart

Purpose
Personal non-commissioned

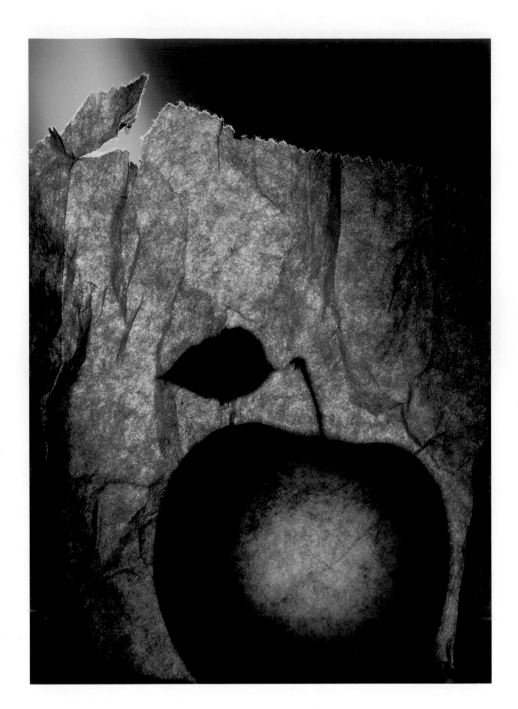

Bob Marchant

Title
Apple
Purpose
Personal non-commissioned
work

John Turner

Purpose
Personal work

PORTFOLIO

Tim Simmons

(pages 328—332)

Title
Virgin Atlantic Calendar
Art Director
Jon Henry
Client
Virgin Atlantic
Purpose
Direct Mail

GOLD
Kodak Limited

MERIT
Kodak Limited

Andreas Heumann *Printer*
Andreas Heumann

MERIT

Kodak Limited

Andreas Heumann　　*Printer*
Andreas Heumann

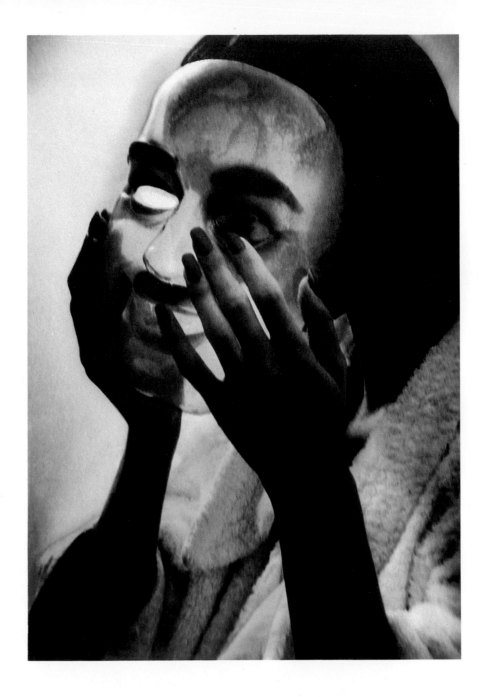

MERIT
Kodak Limited

Andreas Heumann *Printer*
Andreas Heumann

MERIT

Kodak Limited

Andreas Heumann   *Printer*
                             Andreas Heumann

MERIT
Kodak Limited

Andreas Heumann   *Printer*
Andreas Heumann

MERIT

Kodak Limited

Andreas Heumann   *Printer*
Andreas Heumann

MERIT

Kodak Limited

Andreas Heumann   *Printer*
Andreas Heumann

MERIT

Kodak Limited

Andreas Heumann

Printer
Andreas Heumann

MERIT

Kodak Limited

John Claridge

Title
B/W Still Life
Purpose
Personal

MERIT

Kodak Limited

John Claridge

Title
B/W Still Life
Purpose
Personal

MERIT

Kodak Limited

John Claridge

Title
B/W Still Life
Purpose
Personal

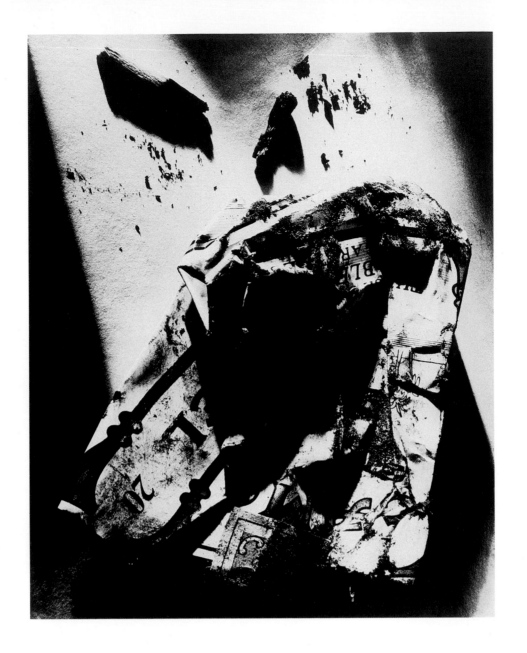

MERIT

Kodak Limited

John Claridge

Title
B/W Still Life
Purpose
Personal

MERIT

Kodak Limited

John Claridge

Title
B/W Still Life
Purpose
Personal

MERIT

Kodak Limited

John Claridge

Title
B/W Still Life
Purpose
Personal

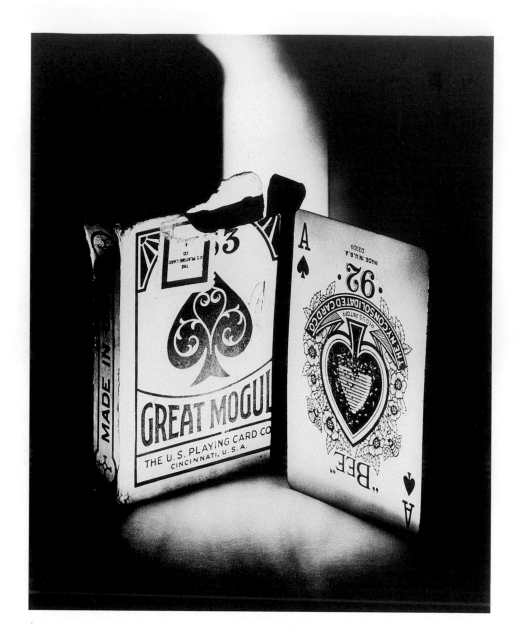

MERIT

Kodak Limited

John Claridge

Title
B/W Still Life
Purpose
Personal

MERIT

Kodak Limited

John Claridge

Title
B/W Still Life
Purpose
Personal

MERIT

Kodak Limited

John Claridge

Title
B/W Still Life
Purpose
Personal

MERIT

Kodak Limited

John Claridge

Title
B/W Still Life
Purpose
Personal

SF179

defined by H.M. Government

ISEASE Health Departments' Chief Medical Officers

The designer's dream...come true

No, you're not dreaming – this advertisement is for real. Graphic Books International Ltd offer you a book selection and service second to none wherever you are in the world.

Our 64 page colour catalogue features the top 200 books from our extensive list of professional design, artwork, illustration, photography and reprographics books – all stocked in bulk in our UK distribution centre to cater not only for the thousands of orders from individuals and commercial companies but also the volume requirements of trade outlets and educational organisations.

A single annual payment of just £5* brings you by first class or airmail post a copy of our latest catalogue and a one year subscription to our quarterly book news magazine that will keep you right up to date with new books, the latest annuals and special offers.

For full details of the graphic books mail order service you've always dreamt about but not yet experienced write today, stating the name of the publication in which you saw this advertisement to:–

GRAPHIC·BOOKS INTERNATIONAL

P.O. Box 349, Rue des Goddards, Guernsey, Channel Islands. (U.K.)

(U.K. Distribution Centre: P.O. Box 1, Arndale Road, Littlehampton, W. Sussex, England)

*Applies to overseas requests only (catalogues are free to U.K. customers) and includes a £5 book voucher which can be exchanged against subsequent book orders over £50.
Please make cheques payable to 'Graphic Books' in pounds sterling. Alternatively, payment can be made
by Eurocheque, Access (MasterCard/Eurocard), Visa or American Express quoting the card number, cardholders address and expiry date.

J e r r y   H o a r e

(0222) 49 8605

will barton

Reading (0734) 67707

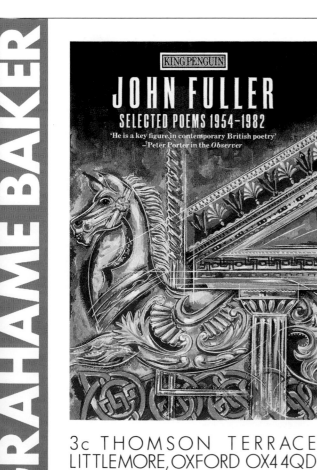

GRAHAME BAKER

3c THOMSON TERRACE
LITTLEMORE, OXFORD OX4 4QD
TELEPHONE: OXFORD 0865 714411

Sorry...

...but however high your profile in the design industry, at Graphics World we don't care about the size of your salary, the car you drive, or the suit you wear. What we do care about is providing you with the kind of information which is going to be useful to you in your work, helping you to justify the salary which pays for the car you drive, the suit you wear, etc., etc.

◆ Typography ◆ Typesetting ◆ Illustration ◆ Reprographics ◆ Electronic page composition ◆
◆ Computer graphics ◆ TV graphics ◆ Printing techniques ◆ Holography ◆ Education ◆ Packaging ◆
◆ Animation ◆ Darkroom techniques ◆ Signage ◆

The £15.00 price tag for an annual subscription needs no apologies – but for those who like to see exactly what they're getting, write or phone for a complimentary copy.

Graphics World Publications Ltd
7 Brewer Street Maidstone Kent ME14 1RU England
Telephone (0622) 686126 (subscriptions)

Annual subscription: U.K. £15.00, Europe £20.00, overseas £20.00, overseas airmail £30.00.

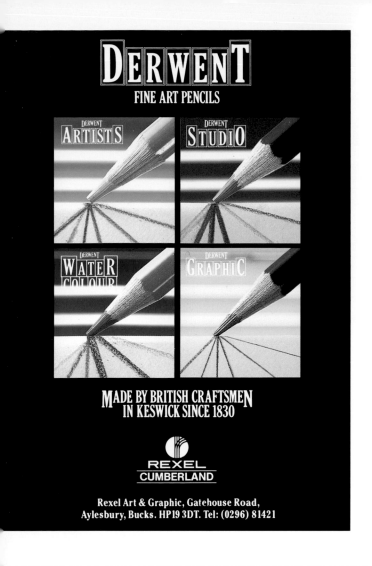

Illustration for
The Listeners, Walter de la Mare

Shirley Walker

Vicki Thomas Associates
22 Hickman Close
Fulmer Rd., London E16 3TA
(01) 476 3086
Telex: 334003   REF: 42268

ALAN BAKER 0273 32333

ASSOCIATION OF FASHION, ADVERTISING AND EDITORIAL PHOTOGRAPHERS

CREATES

STANDARDS OF PRACTICE, CODES OF CONDUCT,
CONTACTS WORLD WIDE, AN INTERNATIONAL
MEMBERSHIP, FRIENDLY COMMUNICATIONS

PUBLISHES

INFORMATION BOOKLETS, MODEL TERMS,
A HELPFUL MONTHLY MAGAZINE,
A RECOMMENDED MILEAGE CHART, LISTINGS OF
PROP HIRE PLACES, MODEL MAKERS,
NEW STUDIOS, CAR HIRE STUDIOS, ETC

HELPS WITH

CAREERS AND PEOPLES' FUTURES,
STUDIO SHARES, SORTING OUT COMPLAINTS,
FREE LEGAL ADVICE, STUDENTS' PROBLEMS,
GOOD ADVICE, FINDING ASSISTANTS,
HOME ECONOMICS, ODD PROPS, CARNETS,
PINK ELEPHANTS

PROVIDES

UNBIASED ADVICE, INSTANT HELP,
REFERENCE MATERIAL, A PRESS CARD,
A SOURCE OF AID AND COMFORT

BATTLES

WITH PARLIAMENT, ADVERTISING AGENCIES,
MAGAZINE PUBLISHERS, DIRECT CLIENTS,
DHSS, THE UNIONS, SUPPLIERS,
INLAND REVENUE, THE COURTS.

ARRANGES

EXHIBITIONS, COMPETITIONS, AWARDS,
WORKSHOPS, INSURANCE,
DISCOUNTS (HERTZ, AVIS), QUICKER PAYMENTS,
LAST MINUTE PROBLEM SOLVING, STUDIO PAs

OPERATES

A BOOKING SERVICE, A SERVICES BUREAU,
ETHICS DISPUTE COMMITTEE, A GALLERY,
A LIBRARY (IN PLANNING)

AND IS RUN BY
PHOTOGRAPHERS FOR PHOTOGRAPHERS.
FOR INFORMATION RING

01-608 1441/5

Monet by Kodak.

Kodak Films.
The standard for professional photographers.